Curriculum Planning
And
School Psychology

The
Coordinated Approach

BY
DOROTHY S. ROSENBAUM, Ph.D.
School Psychologist, Newfane Central
School, Newfane, New York
AND
CONRAD F. TOEPFER, Jr., Ed.D.
Assistant Professor of Education
State University of New York at
Buffalo, Buffalo, New York

*HERTILLON
PRESS*

*BOX 1677
BUFFALO, N.Y.*

HERTILLON PRESS
Box 1677
Buffalo, N.Y.

CURRICULUM PLANNING AND SCHOOL PSYCHOLOGY

THE COORDINATED APPROACH

Dorothy S. Rosenbaum, Ph. D.
Conrad F. Toepfer, Jr., Ed. D.

TABLE OF CONTENTS

CURRICULUM PLANNING AND SCHOOL PSYCHOLOGY
THE COORDINATED APPROACH

by
Dorothy S. Rosenbaum
Conrad F. Toepfer, Jr.

INTRODUCTION: A STATEMENT OF PURPOSE

Vitalization of curriculum and instruction has long been considered necessary in creating a better school program serving the needs of all the pupils the school is obligated to teach. Such vitalization has been impaired, however, in one way at least, by the fact that traditionally the curriculum supervisor and school psychologist have functioned independently in the public school setting. As a consequence, the failure to coordinate the services of the curriculum supervisor and school psychologist resulted in a failure to recognize what the roles of these two specialists could be, and what their special functions could lead to in the establishment of a cooperative program serving the entire school system.

In coordinating the special training and abilities of the curriculum supervisor and the school psychologist, a greater vitalization of the all-school program could be achieved without revolution. As 'such, **"THE COORDINATED APPROACH"** could better utilize all the facilities of the instructional staff through a program of planning and experimentation which takes advantage of the special abilities of each contributing member of the school staff and which leads to the recognition and understanding of the kinds of problems existing within both the school setting, the instructional staff and the pupils themselves.

The function of this program, while not entirely new in all its ramifications, is one that may serve to meet the needs of different school systems serving different kinds of pupils. Although what is to be presented in this text is the special approach which was developed within the Newfane Central School in Newfane, New York, the authors do not expect that this material must be limited to a school system resembling that one. It is anticipated and hoped that what is written here will serve to focus attention on the need to coordinate more and more the efforts of the various specialists in all school settings to the end that such coordination might have lasting value to the pupil and the community in which he lives. It is the conviction of the authors that "THE COORDINATED APPROACH," as developed in this text, is a program of coordination of these specialties within the all–school setting and that it can be adapted by any school having the services of a trained curriculum supervisor and school psychologist. The institution of this program should be based upon the recognition of the need for greater coordination of the all–school program and is accessible to many school situations in that it entails no additional significant financial outlay.

The purpose of this particular coordinated effort may be thought of as preventive in nature. It is hoped that through this approach there will be greater efficiency in using all the special services available within the school system towards the one objective, that of creating a better educational climate for pupils and teachers and, therefore, the community. As such then, there are two areas of prevention which play an integral role in the purpose of this approach.

First of all, it is expected that many of the problems of adjustment that pupils present repeatedly in the traditional school system will be eliminated or alleviated. Most apparent is increased awareness of the difficulty schools appear to be having maintaining the interest and motivation of those pupils who as they approach sixteen become potential dropouts. Many of these pupils,. it has been noted and documented elsewhere, are intellectually capable of considerable achievement. However, many years previous to the time when a pupil feels leaving school is the only solution to whatever his delemma may be, the observing teacher notes a decrease in the child's interest in school, a change in attitude regarding school in terms of achievement and perhaps behavior, and it is in these early years that there is a greater chance of changing the negative to the positive. This can be achieved by creating a setting for him which makes what he learns meaningful in terms of how he lives.

The second area of prevention involves the special problems which teachers develop over the years as they teach. It is well known that teachers often become extremely frustrated by their inability to achieve the goals they set for themselves and for their pupils. Often too, they become anxious and defensive because of the attacks that are constantly directed at them by those who feel teachers have failed to meet the needs of pupils and society. This tends to make some of them at times rigid and inflexible, while others become so flexible that they retain little frame of reference. It is hoped and expected that through this coordinated effort it will be possible to develop greater sensitivity on the part of the teachers to the pupil–teacher interaction, to the needs which pupils have, to the needs which teachers have, and to the recognition that within the interaction between these two groups there must be sensitive understanding and the recognition of the needs for developing a far more meaningful learning situation. Furthermore, through a more sensitive and perceptive teacher–pupil interaction, teachers may be helped to develop a more realistic perception of the child as an ever changing person with values and attitudes, hopes, ideals, and aspirations which may be distinctly different from those which they would hold for themselves. Herein lies the true meaning of the worn–out phrase – "individual differences" – to which teachers must give more than lip service.

Finally, it is intended that this coordinative effort will give greater incentive to the entire student body and faculty for the development of creative experiences which are not purely academic or sterile in the academic sense, but experiences which involve all of life and living, experiences thus, which are of real value to all. The purposes of "**THE COORDINATED APPROACH**" are not new to the objectives of the American public educational setting. Newness, or if we must call this by name, originality, lies in the utilization of specialists on hand in a majority of our school systems in such a way as to capitalize on available facilities and talents without the expenditure of more than creative energy.

The style in which this text is presented will, in some instances, be narrative in terms of the actual experiences of the authors as the program evolved. In other instances, it will be expository in terms of identification of situations, analyses, and recommendations. It is hoped that this variation of style will help clarify the manner in which "**THE COORDINATED APPROACH**" evolved as well as the scope which it may attain.

CHAPTER I

DEVELOPMENT OF
"THE COORDINATED APPROACH"

A. The Role of the Curriculum Supervisor and the School Psychologist

In introducing a definition and description of the curriculum supervisor and the school psychologist as they developed within the Newfane setting, the reader may arrive at the conclusion that the functions of these two specialists overlap to such a degree as to eliminate individual functioning within the individual specialty. Such a depreciation of individual function has not occurred. Rather, it is felt by the authors that their close cooperation in "THE CO-ORDINATED APPROACH" has resulted in a clearer identification of what specific functions each specialist should separately retain.

Within the Newfane school setting, the school psychologist served the entire K through twelfth grade program with designated system-wide responsibility, while the curriculum supervisor had designated responsibility only in the secondary program, grades seven through twelve. While this has precluded bilateral participation by both specialists in implementing "THE COORDINATED APPROACH" at both elementary and secondary levels, both authors were able to cooperatively plan both the elementary and secondary aspects of the program. As later recommendations will specify, expansion of the program to all levels should be predicated upon both specialists' operating with designated K through 12, or system-wide responsibility.

It should be remembered that while "THE COORDINATED APPROACH" did not evolve bilaterally at all levels, it has become operational at all levels and has achieved a definite system-wide impact. Without the loss of individual function in the two specialties involved, each of the specialists considers his roles as having expanded to cover tangential functioning, so that even individual functioning has not occurred in isolation.

The functions of supervision and curriculum coordination, originally roles of the school administrator, have evolved into functions which have increasingly been delegated to specially trained personnel who in turn are responsible to the school administration. While both of these functions have developed to the point of generally being delegated to such trained personnel, the school administrator has continued to retain some aspects of the supervisory role due to his legally defined position as the responsible leader of the instructional staff. The administrative aspect of the supervisor's tasks have remained definitely more recognizable within line–staff relationships because of the evaluative implications of the supervisor's role in hiring and firing of staff.

On the other hand, the administrative delegation of functions of curriculum coordination has generally resulted in a greater gulf between the perceived tasks of the administrator and those of the curriculum coordinator than has been true with regard to the administrator and the supervisor. While the improvement of the instructional program of the school necessitates a coordinated interaction among administrators, supervisors and curriculum coordinators, the tasks of the curriculm coordinator have become more specialized and in terms of line–staff perceptions, viewed as distinctly separate from the administrative–supervisory level.

While the operational patterns of the supervisor and the curriculum coordinator differ greatly in various sections of the United States, these two functions have, for the most part, remained specialized and delegated to separate positions within the school setting. Curriculum and supervisor theory both have grown to concur that these two functions should continue to be separately assigned for optimal operational effectiveness.

Theory views this effectiveness as follows: The curriculum coordinator, in his objective to improve the quality of instruction through new curricula, reassessed and reorganized programs, more meaningful instructional materials, and improved implementation of instructional techniques, is considered to operate most effectively as a consultant to the faculty. In order to maintain this position as consultant, a confidential relationship between teacher and coordinator and among teacher groups and coordinator must be developed if teacher problems are to be candidly brought to the coordinator for his introspection and recommended approaches for solution. Failure of this confidential relationship to develop can result in considerably less than an honest exposition of teacher instructional and curricular problems to the coordinator and hence, in his resultant inability to function at an effective level. Typically, the delegation of supervisory functions as well as curriculum coordinative functions to the same specialist has contributed to teacher apprehension of this person's supervisory roles and has often convinced the teacher to be considerably less than candid in revealing his instructional problems to the same person when he attempts to function in a consultant role as curriculum coordinator.

While relatively infrequent, there have been some successful situations in which both supervisory and curriculum coordinative functions have been vested in a single specialist. Such situations have developed in comparatively unique settings, however, and because of the unpredictability of such infrequent successes, theory and experience generally recommend separate delegation of these functions. While the position of secondary curriculum supervisor involved combining the functions of curriculum coordination and supervision, it was possible in this situation to develop the emphasis on curriculum coordination while sharing the evaluative functions with administration. Thus, the actual functions of the curriculum supervisor emphasized curriculum development activities.

Various attempts have been made to define the role of the school psychologist in the public schools of the United States. Obviously since so many attempts at definition have been made and continue to be made, no particular definition has been satisfactory to the great majority of practicing school psychologists. That this is so may reflect difference in training, in supervision, in school population, and certainly, in school administration. That differences in role definition exist between school psychologists, however, does not necessarily reflect disagreement as to what should be or needs to be done in our schools. This disagreement may lie in the emphasis and in the time allocated to the various functions the school psychologist performs.

It is not intended here to review the history of the development of school psychology. This has been done extensively elsewhere and need not be repeated here. However, a short review of the history of school psychological services in the Newfane Central School, probably recapitulates the history of school psychology in general. It may have value to the reader as a means of observing the developmental definition of the school psychologist's role in this small, neither rural nor suburban community. Until 1958, Newfane had no school psychological services at all. Since there were no classes for retarded children, diagnosis of such children served no more than an academic purpose, and, therefore, retarded children and those suspected to be retarded, were not seen at the initiation of the school. Previous to this date, however, emotionally disturbed children were seen by one or the other of the two community child guidance clinics. One of these clinics did regularly consult with school personnel, making suggestions concerning the handling of a particular child. These consultations were generally held with the guidance counselor. The other clinic occasionally sent a report to the school but personal contacts were not arranged.

In 1958, anticipating the development of a special class for retarded children, the Newfane Central School sought the services of a school psychologist on a consulting basis. Services were essentially testing, with little if any opportunity to discuss the findings with either the parents or the faculty. One of the authors, in assuming this position, was quite frustrated by the complete lack of closure on any pupil because of the lack of intake and interpretive parent conferences, or teacher conferences to gain school behavioral history or to discuss the findings and recommendations. The opportunity to follow up any of the youngsters was completely lacking and in 1960, arrangements for psychological consulation were changed.

With the psychologist serving the schools only 50 days during the school year rather than on an "as needed" basis, the services were not extended to a greater number of children, but the nature of the services changed. A concerted effort was begun at this time to educate the faculty to the recognition as early as possible, not only of deviant learning and behavioral patterns present in some youngsters, but of the meaning and value of the psychological evaluation. This was done through individual teacher conferences concerning each of the children tested. Pre- and post-testing parent conferences were held with the parents whenever possible, depending entirely upon parental cooperation. In some instances, even repeated phone calls and letters did not elicit such cooperation, but generally, such efforts were rewarded. The psychologist also spoke before parent groups in an attempt to inform the community about her work and its purpose. In addition, the psychologist was responsible for the composition of the special class and worked closely with the teacher around each child's special assets and liabilities.

The school administration was quick to respond to the psychologist's statements concerning an effort to institute a preventive program, since referral services for children with behavioral disturbances were not readily available. One of the two child guidance clinics which had earlier served the school was no longer in existence and the remaining clinic had a long waiting list. With the blessing of the administration, psychological services to this system of approximately 2,600 pupils were extended to 100 days out of the school year in 1962 and to 120 days in 1963, and the progłum described in this text went into effect.

The role of the school psychologist, as these writers see it, primarily involves focusing upon the prevention of school problems rather than their "cure." This definition stems from the universal problem of the lack of time for the psychologist to be everything to all men and the lack of readily available therapy services, private and public, in a relatively isolated neither rural nor suburban community. The need for treatment facilities is obvious and need only be mentioned here. To institute a therapy service within this particular school would so cut into the psychologist's already limited time that all of the services would be markedly curtailed and it changes the school's emphasis and responsibility. Focus on prevention, it was hoped, would eventually produce the desired results of a decrease in school problems and thus markedly lessen the need for prolonged treatment of such children. In addition, this kind of focus stresses and uses the entire school staff.

This focus defined the role of the psychologist in the following way. Prevention was to be attacked through a three-directional effort. This effort would involve teacher in-service education, early diagnosis, and parent education. Teacher in-service education appeared to hold the greatest opportunity for the prevention of pupil problems, either of a learning nature or those primarily involving behavior. At the onset, since early diagnosis is so crucial, it was felt that emphasis at the primary and elementary level could go a long way in alleviating those problems which develop because of neglect. This meant also that the teachers needed to see the importance of their behavior, especially as manifested by their attitudes towards their pupils and their understandings of those pupils, and how their behavior might be reflected in their classrooms.

Two approaches were worked out. One involved close communication with the teacher during all stages of a referral and especially after the child's diagnosis was completed. The second involved a relatively formal series of workshops in which a number of different, but common classroom problems and techniques could be discussed. The former approach is immediately rewarding to the teacher, because she sees that her referral has been dealt with and any results or recommendations regarding her role are shared with her. Her interest in the child is accepted professionally and she is given whatever help is available (and considerable personal support) – all of which reward her efforts to serve and refer so that she may teach. The workshop series attacks the problems inherent in the backgrounds of these teachers whose knowledge of human development and observations of development left them with less than adequate ability to detect and observe carefully those children who might need special help. In addition, discussions of various classroom techniques, it was hoped, would bring out into the open a greater understanding of those techniques, including their assets and liabilities.

Emphasis on early diagnosis was obviously related to the workshops. However, to encourage referral in the early grades, the psychologist spent considerable time observing in kindergarten and the first grade and a number of possible problems were discovered in this way. It was felt that teachers would soon take the initiative themselves and screen their youngsters where they had not done so before.

The third direction of effort was aimed at parent education. This was not limited to speaking at P.T.A. meetings or Mothers' Clubs. Teachers were encouraged to communicate with parents wherever problems might be brewing. Parents were informed by the teachers of the availability of the school psychologist for consultation and referral and were encouraged to contact the psychologist themselves if they suspected a problem which might reflect itself in behavioral disturbance not necessarily seen in the school situation. It was hoped that in making known the availability of the school psychologist, parents would in time become not only more aware of what could be done to help their children, but would also become less likely to think of referral as representing "the end of the world" for them.

With the development of closer relationship with the teachers, further avenues of prevention became apparent. These involved a greater concern with curriculum and teacher adjustment. In the former area, the psychologist felt the need of considerable help from the curriculum supervisor. Knowing what subject matter was being taught at the various grade levels was not enough. Definition of objectives and clarification of the relationship between content and the needs of pupils had to be considered. Here it was apparent that there was considerable likelihood of duplicity of the services of both the school psychologist and the curriculum supervisor with the possibility of working at opposite ends. This led to a need felt by both the authors to plan together. Out of a discussion concerning curriculum, further areas of mutual concern became apparent and the ideas presented in this text evolved.

B. Overlap of Function

The concept of "THE COORDINATED APPROACH" received its initial stimulus from some compatible and mutual interests of the curriculum supervisor and school psychologist. Out of several initial meetings, the authors came to considerable agreement concerning problems which the school system faced in developing a realistic all-school program.

The first of these was seen to be the lack of functional cooperation of all faculty and staff in achieving efficient communication within the school setting. Because of this inadequacy in communication, various components of this system remained isolated, uninformed and therefore relatively incapable of efficient and intelligent operation. Wasted motion in terms of overlap of function and duplication of effort as well as gaps in areas of function which remained unnoticed and neglected, continually haunted many aspects of the all-school program. One cardinal instance of this involved the traditional operation of the specialized services, especially the school psychologist and the curriculum supervisor. The former area of specialization seeks to help students make an optimal adjustment to the all-school program. The area of curriculum planning seeks to plan, implement, evaluate, and reorganize this all-school program to be as effective as possible in terms of meeting the needs of the student at each level of his development.

The American public school has witnessed the eager and spontaneous fluctuation and movement of both areas of specialization with some progress, some retrogression and some marked achievements. Traditionally, however, both of these specialized functions have operated with relatively no recognition that cooperative planning of their respective functions might weave a strong fabric of experience for students. It is felt that schools have suffered from the lack of cooperation in coordinating the special talents of these specialists and that this lack of communication between any two or more major services within a school setting has led to duplication of services, misunderstanding, etc. Confusion on the part of the teacher was a readily observed result, since for example, the teacher was often caught in the middle between curriculum planning and expectation of the curriculum supervisor and the modification of curriculum advised by the school psychologist with reference to specific children. It has been suspected that in the lack of this communication between the curriculum supervisor and school psychologist neither has known what the other hoped to accomplish nor how he planned to achieve his goals. By chance they have often struggled toward opposite ends to create gaps in the all-school program. This lack of awareness of inefficiency may seem ludicrous but it is darkly tragic that these areas of specialization have been so myopic in their operational patterns as to be ignorant of their overlap of functions.

The obvious pattern which the authors identified in this was that the curriculum supervisor in his work of planning, reorganizing and vitalization of the program could be much more effective if advantage were taken of the information and reaction of students gained through their involvement with school psychological services. Similarly, the effectiveness of the school psychologist could be enhanced were his operational decisions to be made with greater knowledge of school objectives, programs, and curricula. It was hoped that this "new" approach of cooperative operation between the two areas of specialization would lead to a more realistically planned curricular experience and for alleviation of the adjustment problems of many of those students who are frustrated by contact with programs which formerly were planned independent of the student and his interests.

Initially, the expanded role of the school psychologist was seen to incorporate considerable classroom visitation. This would allow the psychologist, who is the expert in learning in the school setting, to consider the stated difficulties of students in helping the curriculum supervisor evaluate the degree to which curricular experiences realistically did meet the important needs of students. The expanded role of the curriculum supervisor was initially seen as providing opportunity for the psychologist to make such visitations and to plan to work closely with the psychologist and other pupil personnel services in reviewing and reorganizing the curriculum to incorporate more effectively pupil needs and school objectives.

The beginning attempts to implement "**THE COORDINATED APPROACH**" as expressed in the previous paragraph allowed both specialists to arrive at additional mutual understandings in organizing their initial ideas. Most of these ideas centered about developing more classroom experiences in relation to stated objectives. In a majority of instances, the objectives pointed to the identification of felt pupil needs. However, many of the experiences developed from these objectives frequently lost considerably in the translation! Observations led to the identification of these school-wide problems which typically have been independently pursued by curriculum workers and school psychologists with varying degrees of duplicity and omission in functioning. The most critical of the problems, which flourish within those areas of overlap, are listed as follows:

I.   Problems Focusing on the Instructional Staff

A.   **Poor Communication**
     Teachers often failed to realize that communication is more than verbal. Even in instances where teachers realized this difficulty, their level of communication was not on a level which facilitated student understanding. The differences between values of teachers and students created other communication problems. Teacher unawareness of these differences as well as what the values of students actually were contributed considerably to ineffective communication.

B.   **Lack of the Consideration of the Nature of Learning**
     Teachers largely seemed to plan their teaching independent of what they thought learning was and how it

took place among students. Most teachers when asked what they considered the nature of learning to be were actually quite confused and had no frame of reference or experience for organizing a response.

C. Awareness of the Nature of the Student

Teachers were not aware of the systematic differences between younger and older adolescent students, nor were they aware of basic sex differences. The tendency to approach these groups similarly made for difficulties in gaining and holding interest and attention. Lack of such awareness placed the emphasis of their teaching on subject matter and content without regard for what meaning this held for their students.

II. Problems Focusing on the Student

A. Inadequate Background

Evidence indicates that students are often inadequately prepared for their entrance into the secondary program. Remedial programs which might well be appropriate here, are often neglected since it is felt by many teachers that it is too late to provide remedial work at the secondary level or that such work is not part of the function of the secondary school.

B. The Problem of Individual Differences

Readiness to assume the responsibility for high school work is too often assumed and taken for granted by teachers. Students suffer when they are all expected to be ready to learn from the same experience at the same time. Similarly harmful is the false assumption that everything to which students are exposed by the teacher is meaningful. Individual differences encompass differences in intellectual, emotional, physical and social abilities. These differences at the secondary level are often hidden in the student's effort to conform to the peer group.

C. Relationship with Authority

This is an area of tremendous concern to the student in his effort to become independent without surrendering his dependence. This is a problem closely related to learning but is quite often construed by the teacher to be totally unrelated, if it is considered at all.

D. **Incentive and Motivation**

Students have a drive to learn but what is often taught them serves to frustrate this drive. That this frustration interferes with learning affords an excellent rationale for the student's not being motivated enough to learn.

E. **Community Influence**

Learning is most effective if it can satisfy a personally defined goal. To establish goals which cannot be realistically satisfied within the environment of the community in which the student lives indicates that the school functions in a vacuum. Failure to meet the needs of a community, present and future, further serves to discourage learning because the student finds in his community no place to apply that which he has learned and soon the goals of the school program have no real meaning.

The identification of these foregoing areas of problems was arrived at by the curriculum supervisor and the school psychologist and gave the curriculum supervisor important areas for consideration in his work with the staff. It also provided impetus at the secondary level to the preventive focus of the school psychologist.

From the identification of the kinds of problems with which the school is concerned, the overlap of function between the areas of responsibility of the curriculum supervisor and the school psychologist became evident. It was felt that any overlap of functions or gaps in functions resulting in confusion and duplication of effort, or failure to identify important problems in the all-school program, indicated a need for coordination. While each of the specialists possessed skills which would enable him to effectively attack to some degree each of these problems separately, the coordinated efforts added up to a "whole" larger than the sum of its parts. As an example, the school psychologist is constantly reminded that adolescence is often a period of stress and strain. To recognize that this stress exists in part as a function of a struggle with authority, the failure of subject matter to meet the needs of the community and the student, is only a portion of solving the problem. In "**THE COORDINATED APPROACH**," the school psychologist draws on his knowledge of the student as a human being and coordinates this with the curriculum supervisor's knowledge of the curriculum. If there is a discrepancy between what the teacher deems to be the importance of the curriculum and the student's perception of the curriculum, then this discrepancy serves to block communication. The curriculum supervisor is the instructional specialist, and when his knowledge of curriculum is coordinated with the psychologist's knowledge of the student, the "whole" truly does equal more than the sum of its parts! From this recognition and evaluation of the special skills of each of the two specialists, "**THE COORDINATED APPROACH**" evolved.

C. Initial Ideas

With recognition of the existence of overlap of functions and gap in functions, the authors set out to consider what could be done to make working together a realistic and effective procedure. It may seem strange to the reader, but neither the curriculum supervisor nor the school psychologist really knew what the special skills of the other were. At the same time, the authors knew what the skills of each were generally reputed to be. Discussing them openly helped each to understand not just what the other could do, but what he could not do. Actually, communication between the authors, as specialists in their respective fields, became highly effective as the identification of each other's specific skills increased.

It became apparent that the curriculum supervisor and the school psychologist held a common goal, the provision of an educational climate conducive to the nurturing and development of each child's experiences, assets, and skills to the limit of his ability. With the identification of this common goal, it became necessary to analyze what their special skills were and what means they could utilize to achieve this stated goal.

Obviously, the curriculum supervisor must have a thorough grounding in curriculum requirements as they pertain to subject and content matter. But this is hardly sufficient to meet the goal of education set forth above. Traditionally, the "coordination" toward which the curriculum supervisor has worked has involved the subject matter or academic curriculum of the school. Growing "lip-service" has been given to Krug's definition of the expanded concepts of curriculum, holding that the curriculum consists of all those experiences which the child undergoes through the direction of the school within the school day.[1] However, few schools have made this definition operational. It should be apparent that the concept of meaning must be closely correlated with whatever curriculum turns out to be. Meaning, however, depends upon the child's individual intellectual and emotional development as well as on his social-cultural background, each of which helps or hinders the development of motivation, his concept of meaning, and his perception and pursuance of the goals of education.

[1]Krug, Edward A., **Curriculum Planning,** Harper and Brothers, New York, New York, second edition, revised, 1957., pp. 1-4.

To this end then, the second highly specialized skill of the curriculum supervisor should be a solid grounding in the field of growth and development, the dynamics of inter-personal relationships and human learning in education. Curricular experiences organized without a basic awareness of these areas can have little more than rote applicability to the child for whom it is intended. This kind of uncorrelated curriculum serves the purpose of perpetuating the false notion that each child in our society receives an equal education because all children are exposed to the same subject matter!

The third skill which the curriculum supervisor must possess is directly related to the supervision of teachers. Teachers have a magnificent opportunity to sell what they teach so that the child makes a genuine effort to buy. Unfortunately, as is often suspected if not completely substantiated, teachers frequently fail to come across with the goods. This failure may result from the teacher's preoccupation with one or a combination of the following: his over-concern with subject matter to the exclusion of everything else, his over-concern with something else to the exclusion of subject matter, and his attitude about himself and about his pupils, which attitude, of course, reflects his expectations of himself and others.

Supervision of teachers is not a simple matter. This is true partly because the teacher's role and how well that role is performed has never been clearly defined in terms of either the pupil's expectations of his teachers or for that matter, the teacher's expectations of himself. Evaluations of a teacher's performance as a teacher also have never been concretized and often this evaluation remains such a highly abstract process that neither teacher, pupil, parent, nor supervisor can in any way operationally justify the opinion he has reached. Nonetheless, the curriculum supervisor must be well prepared to fulfill his functions in the supervision of the instructional program. He can supervise because he knows curriculum content, instructional materials, methodology and techniques of instruction, and the pupils for whom the curriculum is intended. Thus, three of the specific areas of skill of the curriculum supervisor include knowledge of curriculum, knowledge of people, and knowledge of coordinative and supervisory functions. Obviously, the grounding of the curriculum supervisor in human growth and development is important in achieving these ends. However, the specialized training of the school psychologist can and does give an expertness to much of the curriculum supervisor's tasks which require thorough knowledge in the area of human learning.

The psychologist, to function effectively within the school setting, must also be well versed in a number of areas. Since there are not many schools which can afford to hire both clinical and educational psychologists, the school psychologist must serve in some way as a combination of these two areas of specialization. The skills of the clinical psychologist lie primarily in the areas of psychodiagnostics and psychotherapy. He is trained to work with people of diverse ages to determine the nature and extent of the adjustment difficulties, and in these relationships, especially to the child of school age, to his functioning within the school situation. Thus, he is trained to evaluate intellectual abilities and achievement and to appraise personality at various levels of depth. He is skilled in interview techniques and utilizes these in dealing with the child and his parents.

In most school settings, psychotherapy is not offered to the child by the school psychologist. There are a number of reasons for this which need not be discussed here. However, recommendations of a therapeutic nature are primarily directed to the parents, and those which can fit the school setting are directed to the teachers who deal with the child. These may involve environmental manipulation within the school, i.e., a change of classrooms or teachers, modifications in teacher–pupil relationships, concern with setting of limits, etc. While the school psychologist can typically suggest modifications within these areas in the instructional program, he cannot be very specific here because he usually lacks background in subject matter and content areas unless these relate primarily to his own specialized field of mental health, a field which is not generally open to school age pupils as subject matter. Thus, unless he has had specific training within the field of teacher education, he must be general as far as subject matter and content modifications are concerned.

It is quite likely that educational psychologists are most concerned with educational tests and measurements as these may be developed for use in the school setting. However, it is expected that the educational psychologist has a greater grounding than does the clinical psychologist in the psychology of education. This suggests that the educational psychologist has a better or at least a broader background than does the clinical psychologist in the functioning of the child within the classroom situation in terms of educational techniques, the concepts of reward and motivation, and the aspect of subject and content matter as it involves particular pupil learning situations. Thus, the educational psychologist meshes beautifully with the clinical psychologist in terms of a more thorough appraisal of the functioning of the pupil within the entire school system. Now we have the ability to evaluate the pupil, not only in terms of intelligence and personality, but also in terms of achievement and application within the school setting.

As was stated earlier, most schools cannot afford to hire a clinical as well as an educational psychologist. Hopefully, the school psychologist is trained to function as a combination of both. Although often he is not as firmly grounded in the area of personality testing or evaluation as is the clinical psychologist and quite probably not as well grounded as is the educational psychologist in tests and measurements, he does have considerable background in both areas. If he is well trained, he can function as a modified combination of these two areas of specialization.

In recapitulation then, the objective of "THE COORDINATED APPROACH" lies primarily in the area of prevention of learning disability and educational failure. Therefore, the program about to be presented must be sufficiently careful in its planning as to expose the entire K through 12 faculty of the school system to the entire range of experiences which are combined in "THE COORDINATED APPROACH." Prevention is not something that can be defined at a particular age. The only thing which experience verifies here is that prevention means "start early"!

"THE COORDINATED APPROACH" as it has evolved under the efforts of the authors consists of cooperatively planned programs in five areas. These five areas constitute the core of preventive effort. They are:

1. **Classroom visitations.** This allows the school psychologist, as the learning specialist, to observe how the students react to existing operational curricula and the teacher. Subsequent curriculum planning activities can have the benefit of consultation with the school psychologist to gain an interpretation of the needs of curricular programs in terms of key aspects of human learning effectiveness and human relations.

2. **Teacher group therapy.** This allows teachers in groups of eight or ten to focus upon their individual relationships to the curriculum, students, and to each other. Acquiring realistic self–perception can help the teacher accurately assess and improve his total effectiveness in the instructional program.

3. **Review workshops.** This approach to in–service education allows focus to be drawn upon broad educational problems as they exist in the dynamics of the actual individual school situation in which teachers operate. The strengthening of teacher perceptions and the identification of approaches for improving instruction in terms of these problems within the specific school, can be an avenue to dramatic curriculum improvement.

4. **Unit Planning.** This allows the school psychologist, as learning specialist, to contribute to the planning of units of instruction based upon a sound awareness of human learning. This can be strongly preventive in the sense that key problems often result from

curricula typically planned without concern for important learning needs. This can be extended to entire course curriculum planning for special classes which accommodate slow learners, mentally retarded, and physically handicapped students, etc., as well as honors classes.

5. **Consulting teacher services.** This allows the psychologist to bring his specialized knowledge of human behavior into the classroom to explain subject matter content. Analysis of literary content, the direct teaching by the psychologist of aspects of mental health units, and the psychological interpretation of certain material in social studies, all can help students gain an understanding of such subject matter which teacher background is not prepared to offer.

This program will necessitate system–wide provision of curriculum supervisory and school psychological services. In large school systems, it will mean the involvement of several specialists in both areas at the elementary as well as the secondary level.

The purpose of this text is to spell out in as much detail as the authors now have available, what has in effect originated from a single germ of an idea. That idea was not simply that the schools could do a better job, or that they are not doing a good job now. The point, specifically and simply, was that the coordinating of the entire school program, all the special services available, whether they come from school personnel or from outside the school, be brought into the school setting and made a living part of each child's experience, his aspirations, and his achievements. This text, then, will explicate the experience of the authors in developing and implementing "THE COORDINATED APPROACH" with recommendations for refining and extending the program.

The approach is not new in all aspects for certainly it has been thought of by a number of different people in a number of different ways. Rather, it is new in the sense that the two specialists each saw their functions as different and yet as similar and were able to combine their special skills in such a way as to devise what may be considered to be a hopeful, meaningful change in the philosophy of education. It is not simply that each child is to be educated to the best of his ability, nor is it that each child is to be maintained or contained in the school setting until graduation or until he reaches the age when he may legally leave school. It is rather that as long as he is in school, no matter how long that be, that he find school an inspiring experience, not one that takes place out of context of his life but within the context of everything he experiences. This is in essence, then, the objective of "THE COORDINATED APPROACH."

CHAPTER II

THE ALL – SCHOOL PROGRAM

A. Classroom Visitation Program

During discussion, the authors considered their respective functions as psychologist and curriculum supervisor in terms of identifying how their functions might complement each other. The initial consideration of the traditional diagnostic functions of the school psychologist led to the conclusion that even in this traditional field of operation there was an undiscovered area for cooperation by the two specialists. The supervisor, in pursuing his functions of curriculum development, as well as teacher supervision, might be made aware of those student problems and areas of curricular inadequacy which appeared to be significantly contributory to individual student problems identified by the psychologist.

Further exploration of this possibility led to the realization that the failure of the school psychologist to be involved in curriculum planning was a serious waste of training. It seemed almost ludicrous that while the psychologist was the only expertly trained person in Psychology of Human Learning and the study of adolescence, this person was not heretofore utilized in the planning of learning situations for adolescents! Thus, it was decided to attempt to involve the psychologist with this important background in the planning of curricular experiences.

The implementation of this idea, however, required some careful planning. Traditionally, psychologists are perceived as "head shrinkers" who work with disturbed individuals. Bringing the school psychologist into a role outside of this clearly limited area, would require a reorientation of the thinking of teachers and the professional staff at-large. At the same time, the school psychologist, while expert in the areas as outlined, was not specifically oriented to existing curricula and the effect which curricular programs and teachers, in actual operation, might have upon the experiences of students. Thus, the initial steps to be organized and achieved would be the acceptance of the school psychologist in a role dramatically different from the widely held image of the school psychologist as diagnostician, and the development of an operational setting in which the psychologist could observe teachers and classes in action. The latter experience, it was hoped, would give the psychologist frame of reference from which to regard the curriculum in operation as well as a view of teachers in the classroom as they attempt to implement planned curricular experiences. It was hoped that the psychologist would then be better able to become operative in the planning of learning experiences.

A statement from the curriculum supervisor was distributed to faculty members, indicating a desire to achieve a more succinct planning of the all-school program. Also stated was the rationale for involving the school psychologist in curriculum planning and a statement of the reasons why classroom visitation by the psychologist would be beneficial in broadening this specialist's perspectives. The statement was carefully organized to emphasize that the psychologist was observing the teacher primarily as a teacher and not as a personality even though such a distinction might be extremely difficult to make. This statement was submitted to all secondary faculty, asking them to return the statement indicating whether or not they would be willing to see instituted such a program of visitations by the psychologist. Invitations to visit the classes were initially to be issued on a voluntary basis by the teachers. Positive response was almost unanimous.

Initially, the authors began meeting together to examine syllabi, course outlines, programs of instruction and other instructional materials upon which existing curricula in the school had been developed. At the same time, appointments for observation of particular classes and a sample of subject matter areas were made with those teachers who had volunteered for such activity. The supervisor and psychologist made joint visitations which were followed by conferences with the teacher of the class observed. This allowed for an exchange of information which helped teachers, not only to benefit from whatever comments the authors might make, as well as the opportunity to contribute specific information for the background of the psychologist. On a selected basis, the psychologist and supervisor were able to develop a common background in terms of observation of classes, curricular problems observable, areas for improvement as well as areas of strength in the program. Junior high as well as senior high school experiences in general, as well as special education areas, were scheduled so that a cross section of the school's program might provide a background for generalized information. At the same time, areas for specific consideration were identified as well. (The units of study which developed from these specific considerations will be presented further on in this chapter.)

As the program of visitation continued, the psychologist was able to take on a role of consultantship with teachers as well as to the supervisor in the planning of new programs. Finally, within the frame of reference of the classroom visitation experience of the psychologist, the ideas for utilizing the psychologist as a teacher and consultant in a specific area to teachers evolved. Teachers of English inquired as to whether or not the psychologist might be available to discuss the psychological implications of various pieces of literature with their classes. Teachers of health and biology defined other areas in which the psychologist might serve as a guest specialist in their program. While this had been hoped for in the thinking of the authors, in several instances teachers assumed the initiative in asking whether such services might be provided. The curriculum supervisor continued to visit many classes independently in terms of performing his separate functions as consultant and supervisor of instruction, but still scheduled some joint visits with the psychologist to continue their study of the total curricular program of the school. It was felt by the autors, that this program of joint observation should become a regular feature of "THE COORDINATED APPROACH." The continuation of this regularized procedure permitted and encouraged the psychologist to become more definitive in her role in curriculum planning activities. It also provided the supervisor with a source of validation concerning the appropriateness of various instructional techniques as well as of the curricular programs to meet the needs of the students for whom they were organized.

Joint observation, followed as it was by the teacher, supervisor and psychologist discussion led to the identification of a number of common problems that cut across all the classes observed, regardless of subject area, or for that matter, grade level. The most obvious source of concern to the two observers involved some question over whether the meanings given to the subject matter, in terms of actual meaning and implied value, had the same meaning and value for both teacher and students.

Meaning and value both have subjective reference. What an individual considers to be the "meaning" of something is related to his own experiential background. So it is with value. Both concepts are in turn related to need and very likely related to motivation.

Knowing what some of the conflicts of adolescence are helps the teacher understand better the needs of her students. Knowing this should be of inestimable value in predicting what meanings and values might be given to concepts and understandings the teacher wishes to convey.

A couple of examples come to mind. In one class on World

History, taught at the 10th grade level, the instructor was discussing Greek civilization with his class. Involved in this was a discussion of Greek democracy. With this as background, the instructor talked about Socrates, his philosophy and contributions and finally, his death. One of the students became quite perturbed that this remarkable democracy could permit such gross error of judgment and such a miscarriage of justice. The instructor was able to talk with the class about the imperfections of Greek democracy, but he did not carry the discussion to the present day democracy of the student's world. Here was an excellent opportunity, had the instructor had a better understanding of his adolescent student, to tie together for the student his intellectualism and asceticism and to help him see that there has never been a perfect society in spite of the student's need for one, for the adolescent often sees the world in severe contrasts—black and white. The world his parents created is full of imperfection. It is the adolescent who has the vigor and the dream to create a truly perfect world. The teacher would do well to recognize the opportunities offered him by his student's adolescent struggle. Then meanings which were abstractions, which had little value to the students come to life. These are the concerns of the student. They are also the concerns of the teacher. When, these concerns overlap, learning takes on vitality.

A second example is relevant at this point. Much effort and expense is being invested in educating students to the dangers of smoking. And it is probably common knowledge that the adolescent can recite by rote a whole list of the dangers of smoking. Yet, adolescents smoke and there is an increase in the percentage of such smokers. Obviously, smoking meets a need of the student who develops the habit. It's not an addiction to tobacco, at least not at the inception of his habit, so the need must lie elsewhere. Perhaps it lies in the student's need for adult status, for independence, as an expression of his ability and desire to follow his own demands, rather than the desires of adult authority figures around him. If the health teacher and the school nurse teacher would keep in mind what may lie behind the student's acceptance of the cigarette habit, it is at least possible that there will be more meaning to the adolescent of the information he gets about smoking. He must not be told only the dangers of smoking. He must be told the positive aspects as well. (We might add here that this is a far more honest approach especially if the teacher happens to smoke.)

These examples may help the reader see what one of the values of the joint classroom visitations are. The school psychologist does have some special knowledge, especially about the students which the school services. This knowledge should be put to use in the classroom.

B. Teacher Group Therapy

The psychologist author has felt for many years, that any group with an area of common interest could become a therapeutic group under appropriate conditions. Certainly, every classroom has that potential given a certain amount of leadership. And even without special leadership, every observer of a reasonable number of classes will soon find at least one in which the children act in a supportive way to some youngster who stands out as needing help and patience, or they will, en masse, ignore or avoid a particular child for his outbursts. But they will be responding on the basis of their feelings for the child and for the situation. There will be what could produce therapeutic understanding were there some direction and opportunity for interpretation and reflection.

The psychologist has also felt that teachers often have considerable difficulty within their classrooms as a result of their ignorance of human interaction and because of their fears around such interaction. Thus, the psychologist author wanted to introduce into the school setting some kind of teacher group therapy. This, the author felt, might help teachers come to a better understanding of their own roles in the classroom situation, in the give and take of teaching.

In many work situations, things come about by accident or most fortuitous circumstances. Group therapy was an outgrowth of an entirely fortuitous circumstance. The classroom visitations provided a fruitful jumping-off point for the inception of a therapeutic group for teachers since problems of communication and meaning were observed in the classrooms regardless of subject matter.

It will be recalled that the authors were concerned with developing opportunity for the psychologist to become involved in the planning of curricula. They also were concerned with an attempt to determine in what ways the psychologist could help teachers to improve their skills and to develop realizations necessary for improved effectiveness in the organization of instruction. Group therapy for teachers was identified as one approach which might be feasible as a means of achieving such objectives.

The classroom teacher is, like every other human being, affected by his own feelings, by his own frustrations, by his own attitudes, and as he is affected by these, he affects others. Within the classroom visitations, the authors could easily see how communication, for example, was affected by teacher attitudes and feelings of the moment. Certainly, teachers were on many occasions somewhat defensive as a result of their being observed by the curriculum supervisor and the psychologist. This was an understandable feeling, but the teachers seemed little aware of the impact of this defensiveness.

As an outgrowth of the classroom visitations, the psychologist and curriculum supervisor felt it would be helpful if they could come back to the teachers in a group meeting with a statement concerning what they saw to be problems common to each of the classroom situations regardless of content area. Obvious among these common problems was communication. A statement was therefore sent to each of the participating teachers inviting them to meet as a group over coffee and doughnuts to discuss what might be involved in their problems of communication. However, the psychologist had not expected that this would soon become a group therapy situation. This developed strictly by good fortune.

The initial meeting of this group of eight teachers was quite "intellectual." The teachers were very interested in knowing that each of them experienced something which impressed their observers as a potential problem, if not an already existing problem. On an intellectual level. it was not at all difficult to discuss what these teachers felt concerning communication, how they defined it, and their understanding of how it took place. But as they continued to discuss this topic, it became a vehicle which brought the teachers together to consider that they communicated both of themselves and subject matter. At the end of this first meeting the enthusiasm was sufficiently high that the suggestion was made by the psychologist to meet again in two weeks to continue group discussion. The psychologist also felt that the group might well become involved in more personal affiars and that it might be worthwhile to raise the issue of group therapy at this point. This was done and the group's reaction was quite surprising. No one showed any overt resistance to participating as a member of a group in a therapeutic situation, and it was left to be discussed at the next meeting, after the members had thought it over.

At the second meeting, there was considerable exchange concerning types of communication as well as means. The psychologist raised the question, "What did the teachers think they communicated in the Cafeteria line?" (In this particular school setting, the teachers ate in the Cafeteria along with their students and they had to go through the same line. It was customary for the teachers to step ahead of the pupils to the beginning of the line.) What might the teachers be communicating to the students and did the teachers have any awareness concerning the students' feelings about this particular activity? This aroused considerable discussion, some resentment and hostility, and a great deal of defensiveness on the part of the teachers in the group. At the conclusion of this meeting, the issue of group therapy was again raised and the structure of the therapeutic group was explained. Pulling together some of the feelings expressed concerning the Cafeteria line helped the members grasp more fully what would probably take place within the therapeutic group and they decided to continue the meetings as such a group. It was agreed that everything discussed within the group would remain entirely confidential and not be mentioned by any participant outside of the actual group meeting time itself. It was also decided that the group would remain closed to the eight members presently belonging, but that any member of the group had the freedom to withdraw from participation at any time without explanation. The group decided to meet for an hour and fifteen minutes at each session every other week, and to close the meeting at the end of the hour and fifteen minutes, regardless of the level of interest at that time.

This group met a total of ten times during the twenty-week Spring semester. Attendance was nearly perfect and interest and motivation was obviously high. It was apparent that members of the group came to a greater awareness of their own behavior and perceived themselves with increased accuracy at the conclusion of the ten meetings. Some of the teachers came to a greater realization of their individual strengths as teachers as well as their weaknesses, but all of the teachers became far more aware that they could not exist as teachers separate from people.

Perhaps the most significant achievement of this group came through a continuing discussion of their concern about themselves as having to meet two standards of behavior, one applicable to themselves as teachers, and the second applicable to themselves as ordinary people. It is to be remembered that this group was teaching in a small "urban" community. If the teachers engaged in community activities, they were involved with the parents of their students. They felt that frequently they had to be on extra special behavior, careful that they do not let their hair down. This produced defensiveness, resentment, and hostility on the part of the teachers. It was very difficult for many of them to see themselves as humans with the foibles of humans. For this reason, a fair amount of guilt was noted with each teacher around his behavior as a teacher. Being able to discuss these feelings over a period of time, in an accepting situation, seemed to be quite helpful to many of these teachers. They talked with the psychologist leader of the group comfortably about having new insights and a broader perception and more realistic perspective. At the end of the Spring semester the group voluntarily decided to meet again in the same closed group the following Fall.

During this semester, the faculty at-large became increasingly interested in what was taking place at the meetings known only as

"Coffee, Calories, and Consideration." While the discussions of these meetings remained confidential, the teachers participating in the group were obviously enthusiastic about the experience, but yet would not indicate what was transpiring at the meetings. It was decided by the authors that the interest now aroused in the faculty at-large might best be taken advantage of as immediately as possible, and that the achievements of the first group warranted expanding the group therapy concept to involve a second group of teachers. A notice, similar to the one distributed to members of the original group, was put forth at the beginning of the next Fall semester to nine other teachers who had participated in the classroom visitation program, and a second group was organized along this same line. With the old group continuing to meet twice a month, the new group was scheduled to meet on the same day on alternate weeks so that the curriculum supervisor and the school psychologist were involved in group therapy activity for one day each week. In structuring the second group, the authors immediately informed them that this was to be a therapeutic group and not a simple discussion group. There was some reticence on the part of the group members to "let themselves go," but this reticence was discussed at some length and overcome by some of the group members. It was felt that results in this second group were somewhat less successful in the same areas of achievement as in the first group, but this group took a longer time to warm up. Unfortunately, this second group could not continue for the full sessions because the psychologist leader took a leave of absence.

While group therapy situations may be structured in many different ways, the members of the group are most generally aware that within and through the group process, they will learn something about themselves and how they relate to others. The therapeutic essence of the group lies in the interaction of its members. The essence of a good teaching situation **also** lies in this process of interaction. It was recognition of this parallel that served as the goal to be achieved. No attempt was made to get at deep personal problems although the authors are aware of the implications of teacher maladjustment.

One of the peculiarities of the structure of the two groups was the involvement of both authors as participating members. At first glance, the reader informed in the area of group therapy may question the advisability of including the curriculum supervisor as a participating group member. Although his relationship with the teachers was not primarily as a supervising administrator wielding tenure control, he was a supervisor. Thus, in the group situation he could easily have been perceived as a threat. For some people this was true, but it was one of the things considered during the group sessions. In fact, in so openly and honestly discussing this concern, the curriculum supervisor himself gained a much clearer awareness of his own relationship with the teachers, and he came to feel less resistance on the part of certain teachers to working with him in individual contact.

The psychologist, too, gained in her relationship with the teachers participating in both groups. They came to see her as able to accept them with their vagaries and idiosyncrasies and they felt she understood the loads they were carrying. With this freer feeling they were able to relate more honestly to her both in and out of the group. This did not produce a rash of confessions of deeply hidden personal problems, although a couple of the teachers did seek some individual help and were referred to psychological services outside of school personnel. It did, however, lead to greater awareness of pupil problems and there was an increase in referrals for psychological evaluation.

The success of the initial attempts with teacher group therapy led the authors to conclude that insofar as possible, additional groups should be organized. It was hoped that such groups would be introduced at the elementary level. Planning was begun to organize a group for beginning teachers. Not only was the goal of greater awareness of the importance of group interaction set, but it was also recognized that many beginning teachers suffer acutely from new-job pangs and feel themselves overwhelmed and alone. Here might be an opportunity to relieve job-related anxiety and to receive much needed support in a setting in which the new teacher would indeed learn.

Some individuals with whom the psychologist author has talked regarding the efficacy of establishing therapeutic groups in the setting in which the group leader must also function as school psychologist, have doubted that the school psychologist could break through resistances in a reasonable period of time. Undoubtedly there are some advantages to having the group leader be outside the school system. The most obvious is that there would be less threat to the teachers, especially if the school psychologists in a particular school system also served in an advisory capacity to administrators responsible for teacher evaluation. But there are distinct disadvantages to "importing" a group leader. It is well known that each school differs from other schools, not just in pupil statistics, but in school loyalties, relationship with principals, etc. The local school psychologist is much more likely to be aware of certain school idiosyncrasies than the outsider. In addition, honestly facing the threat involved in the psychologist-teacher relationship leads to improved communication between the people involved. Finally, it must be remembered that without adequate motivation, the group will never get moving no matter who the leader is. Motivation, since membership is voluntary, is likely to be good and this should move the group members to discuss and handle their ambivalences.

The authors are convinced that teacher–group therapy is a very meaningful and worthwhile approach to the prevention of certain school–related problems. It is no panacea but realistically is a feasible and inexpensive means of attacking a long ignored area in education in a concrete way. The teacher, unaware in a feeling way of the effects of her interaction with her pupils, is unaware of the most effective tools she has. Unfortunately, too many teachers give only lip service to this notion!

C. Elementary Education Workshops

One of the steps introduced to the elementary education faculty by which it was intended to initiate an effort to coordinate teaching and psychological services exclusive of the coordination called for in dealing with a specific child, was the introduction of a series of review workshops conducted by the school psychologist. These were to serve a number of functions, but two of the primary functions involved a lecture discussion review of child development as such development pertained to education, and the development of a closer teacher–psychologist relationship on a general working level.

The former function––that of providing an in–service review of child development and its relationship to the educational climate–– was easily justified. It is generally accepted that subject matter presented in a meaningful context, where experience is ascribed in both the abstract (teaching) sense and the concrete (working) sense, is subject matter learned best. The abstract no longer is purely abstract, but because connections have been made between the teachings or dissemination of information and the practical application of such abstract information, the material is learned and more likely to be understood by meaning rather than learned by rote. The motivation for attendance at these workshops came through the teachers' recognition that here was a review that would capitalize on the practical working knowledge that teachers had themselves gained, and that in this review was an opportunity to examine concepts that were often earlier unconnected and meaningless (since they were originally learned in the relatively sterile college classroom at the freshman and sophomore levels, with children at the periphery). The practicality of this review through lecture–discussion techniques lay in the teachers' immediate ability to tie the concepts to the children they teach, and within this framework, interest, purpose and motivation can easily be elicited.

The second function, that of developing a closer teacher–psychologist relationship on a general working level has considerable merit. The psychologist is perceived by the parent as an authority figure who can easily be threatening. The parent, who is having difficulty of one kind or another with his child, often feels a sense of guilt, shame and failure and these feelings are by no means comfortable for him. The teacher who has a difficult child to deal with, often considers himself to be at least in part, responsible for the difficulty and as he shoulders a feeling of blame, he resembles the parent. Both parent and teacher, then, in the burden of guilt they carry, whether this guilt is realistic or not, become somewhat anxious and defensive. It then becomes necessary, if the psychologist is to be helpful, for the psychologist to cut through some of these uncomfortable feelings before the child can be helped.

In the workshop series, the face-to-face contact between the teacher and the psychologist allows an interchange that need not be contaminated by guilt or that peculiar sense of discomfort that is sometimes a part of the face-to-face interview over a particular problem child. Instead, teacher and psychologist have an opportunity to get to know each other in a nonthreatening setting, and each can see what the other has to offer. Each sees the other as human; the sense of humor comes out and in a relaxed sense, each can learn more readily from the other.

The series was introduced to the K-3 teachers by a memorandum from the psychologist. This memorandum indicated the nature of the workshop, listed the topics to be discussed and indicated that the meetings were to be held once a month after school, each meeting lasting one and one quarter hours. In addition, the teachers were invited to participate on a voluntary basis.

About a week previous to each meeting, a reminder was sent to all K-3 teachers indicating the particular topic for that week and on the morning of the meeting, an announcement was made by the principal over the public address system.

While attendance was entirely voluntary and teachers might come to as many sessions as they wished, attendance was encouraged whenever possible. Fortunately, the teachers themselves soon became the best advertising agents and attendance averaged about 70% of the K-3 faculty. The principal of one of the schools attended each meeting and attendance by the members of his faculty was somewhat higher than was the case in a second elementary school. However, the meetings were also held in this particular school and this may have had as much affect on attendance as the principal's regular participation.

I. What is Normal and What Isn't?

The first topic had two primary objectives. The first objective was to capture the interest of the teachers so that they would find the meetings worth attending. In this sense, the first topic had to effectively startle the teachers to overcome any inertia they might have. To arouse them so that they would leave the meeting to think about what occurred within the meeting was essential if there was to be any carry-over. The second objective was to relate information regarding this concept of normal so that the information might be usable to the teacher.

To this end, normalcy as a concept had to be viewed culturally and socially as well as through the eyes of the normal curve. The concept of normal or average is a gratifying description when referring to health and physical development, but it often has different meanings when referring to intelligence and development. Thus, not only was the concept viewed differently as it applied to different aspects of human behavior, but it was tied with cultural and social values.

In this first meeting, then, this concept of normal or average was given broad definition, and it was apparent from the response of the teachers that for many of them this was a new look at an old concept.

A very quick review was then given regarding certain aspects of development in children at K-3 level. Motor development, language skills, social patterns and play, were briefly discussed along with attention span, curiosity, and motivation. These were also tied to set differences. These were related to what the teachers see daily in their classrooms and relationship was also drawn to teachers' expectations of their pupils at these age levels.

II. Test Anxiety and Evaluation—Teacher and Pupil

Evaluation has been a problem for teachers for many years. They are concerned with evaluation of pupils not only as such evaluation reflects pupil progress, but also as it reflects teacher ability. In addition, it is extremely difficult to separate from achievement various other aspects that are often evaluated, i.e., effort, attitude, and the like, and of course, the teacher's own perception on a subjective level, of the progress her pupils have made.

Since evaluation is a recurring experience throughout life, the importance of considering it as an end and a process cannot be underestimated.

The objectives of the second workshop meeting were then as follows:

1. to review with the teacher the kinds of evaluation that people undergo during their lives,

2. the meaning in terms of success or failure that may be an end of evaluation, and

3. the process of evaluating with accompanying emotional factors as these may affect performance on an evaluative task.

It is not difficult to draw attention to social pressures around evaluation and with regard to young children, the relationship between being liked, being good, being successful, etc. The teachers quickly drew the inference that early childhood experiences, parental expectation, and social-cultural values were closely related to the anxiety evaluation in school often produces, and at this point, the concept of test anxiety was introduced as it had been recently studied by the psychologist. They were able to see the possibility that anxiety might have facilitative or interfering effects on learning, and in addition they were able to see and discuss the differences between evaluation as an end and evaluation as a process.

III. The Purpose and Nature of Referral to the Psychologist

It may seem to the reader that since it was the school psychologist who led these workshops, that this particular topic would have been first on the agenda of workshop meetings. It was not the lead-off topic because the workshops were not solely intended to invite referrals of children deviant in any way, but as stated earlier, the purpose was to review child development within the framework of the educational climate and to bring about a closer relationship between psychologist and teacher.

By the third meeting, the psychologist felt attention could now be turned toward the psychologist as an agent serving the school in a very special way. However, simply pointing out what the psychologist is trained to do with respect to deviant children did not seem as meaningful an approach as one which could combine this aspect within the framework of the role the psychologist can assume in serving both the teacher and the pupil.

The purpose then of this particular workshop meeting was more than a listing of the skills of the psychologist as well as his limitations. While both these factors were considered, the primary purpose of this session was to direct the attention of the teachers to their responsibility in recognizing the kinds of problems which might be alleviated through parent-teacher-psychologist cooperation.

Obvious problems of acting-out behavior and inadequate achievement were quickly recognized. This was readily seen when learning problems, truancy, behavioral disturbance, and the like were discussed. Greater emphasis was placed on two kinds of problems which do not necessarily readily come to the attention of the teacher.

These were, of course, those represented by the withdrawn and exceedingly shy child and those represented by the child with certain not immediately observable disturbances. With regard to the latter group, there was considerable interest in knowing more about children with neurological problems and chronic minimal brain disfunction.

Within the framework of the referral process, the workshop was directed at helping the teachers recognize the potential value of referral, as well as the process involved in initiating referral. The fact that the psychologist was dependent upon the teacher for help throughout the referral process was pointed out and suggestions were made regarding the preparation of the child, etc. Finally, it was stated that referral to the psychologist, diagnostic evaluation, and parent conference as well as post–evaluation teacher conference would be of little value unless the teacher considered carefully any recommendations made which involved her, and assumed the further responsibility of conferring with the psychologist if the problem was not alleviated to some degree or if the recommendations were inappropriate or threatening to her in any way.

In terms of the teacher–psychologist relationship, this explanation regarding the nature and process of referral helped to clear up the impossible expectation that the child returns from the psychologist's office "cured" of his disturbance. Knowing what the psychologist could and could not do realistically helped the teachers accept the psychologist as no more or less a human than the teacher, and in fact, helped the teachers recognize that the psychologist was not a mystic performing miracles or the carrier of some strange magic wand. In addition, in discussing the process of referral, the psychologist had an excellent opportunity to support the teachers by helping them recognize their own limitations and what might realistically be expected of them.

Thus, this meeting stressed not only a review of the kinds of problems with which the psychologist might offer help, but also, and equally important, what might reasonably be expected to take place as a result of such a referral. This served the very important purpose of emphasizing the mutual relationship existing between teacher and psychologist, and served also to build a more realistic understanding of the abilities and limitations of each specialist involved.

IV. Home–School Communication

The fourth meeting was designed to take advantage of the growing increase in communication between the home and school. Increased contact between these two major influences on children has long been a goal of many schools. This contact has been apparent in the growth of parent-teacher associations, MOM's clubs, Parents' Nights, and the like, and perhaps on a less personal level, through the efforts of school officials and school boards to let the tax paying public know what the schools are trying to do and what the needs of the schools are.

However, public relations in the schools is quite probably more effective if the "relations" are based on positive contact as it is brought home to the parents by the school child. Obviously, when a child returns home from school exuberant about what he has done in school and pleased with his teacher, the parents are more likely to feel the school is doing a good job and more inclined to support it whenever possible. The frequently heard comment, "A school is only as good as the teacher the child has," is not to be lightly treated.

Home-school communication, therefore, seemed a most worthy topic for discussion. From the psychologist's point of view, such communication had to be meaningful and helpful, not only to the child, but also to his parents and his teacher. The notion of **communication** had to be uppermost in the contact between parent and teacher and **not** the creation of a threatening situation. Thus, the introduction of this topic into the workshop series served the objective of calling attention to the purpose and methods of communication.

Obviously, the primary purpose of a meeting between parents and teacher should be that of helping the child to comfortably achieve what he is capable of achieving. Within this framework, much can be accomplished as long as this goal remains uppermost in the teacher's mind. Thus, the evaluation the teacher makes of the parents she meets -- an evaluation she makes whether or not that was her intention -- and the evaluation the parent makes, can lead to a negative meeting in which communication is bound up in defenses and defending, or it can lead to a meeting in which the desire to help create a climate in which the best of education takes place remains the essence of the conference.

The theme of this meeting was not complicated. Keeping the child as the center of interest, different types of communication were discussed along with the advantages and disadvantages of each. Emphasis was on the face-to-face meeting in a setting assuring some privacy and within this setting, it was noted emphatically that discussion should be limited substantially to material relevant to school. Advice regarding the parents, marriage, parent-child discipline, and the like (while all these factors may affect the child) are not appropriately discussed by the teacher. The need is for the teacher to perceive that while she remains an authority, she is not a physician, counsellor, or clergyman.

Therefore, the meeting also stressed an awareness of the teacher's limitations as she communicates with parents, and the teachers were told of the existence of many public and private agencies to which she might suggest parents go, if what the parents indicate is a need for help beyond the focus of the child as a pupil.

Suggestions were made regarding communication with uncooperative parents, overly dependent parents and aggressive parents. The need to communicate to parents whose children are doing well was also considered simply because these parents, just like all of us, appreciate a good word now and then.

One matter of routine communication was discussed because of the fact that this form of communication is indirect. Children often come home, especially at the beginning of the school year, with confusing statements concerning school supplies and classroom rules. Especially with younger children, parents are not always listening seriously, and such children may find it difficult to convince their parents regarding their class rules and needs. Even if it concerns a matter as "trifling" as which mother sends the birthday cookies this week, the communication is important. A number of ways in which indirect communication could be handled was discussed.

V. Psychotherapy and the Educational Climate

An area about which teachers have had little information or considerable misinformation is psychotherapy. It is unbelievable, but painfully true, that many teachers have nothing but a very vague idea about psychotherapy. To present some important information about what psychotherapy is and what is involved in psychotherapy was a major function of this meeting. But of far greater importance was the need to help the teachers recognize that teaching may bear a striking relationship to psychotherapy.

Thus, this meeting was held not to simply disseminate information, but to stress the factor that psychotherapy is in great measure dependent upon the relationship existing between patient and therapist and that teaching is in a very real sense dependent upon the relationship existing between teacher and pupil. The need for learning and relearning to take place is apparent in both the educational setting and the psychotherapeutic one. For such change to occur, there must be understanding and insight, motivation and interest, and the catalyst human relationship which helps supply these components. A further parallel was drawn between the group experience in the classroom and a special form of therapy—group, i.e., which is becoming increasingly more popular.

Finally, certain things the teacher needs to know to assist the therapeutic process when she has a pupil in therapy were discussed. In particular, the discussion stressed the need to set limits as far as possible in conjunction with therapy, the need to create positive success experiences with the child, and the need to understand the ill child's motives and drives as well as his defensive patterns, and, of course, the need to maintain confidentiality.

Again, however, the teacher was helped to realize that unlike the therapist's relationship with the child, where the child is the primary core, hers involves another responsibility, that of teaching the entire class. All too often, the urge to help is so great that only frustration can result. As in so many other situations, the teacher needs to recognize and accept her own limits and in the discussion the teachers were given considerable support regarding this.

VI. Can We Work with the Neither Here Nor There Child?

While the teacher has the training and skills intimate to the techniques of teaching, she often feels the need for a helping hand with new ideas, creative planning and special means of teaching those children who for one reason or another, do not respond favorably to the approaches she may be using. Frequently, she turns to the school psychologist for special assistance in devising teaching techniques, turning to the psychologist not because of the teaching skills the psychologist possesses but because he has specific training in the dynamics of learning and behavior. It is in the meshing of the teaching skills of the teacher and the knowledge of behavior that the psychologist possesses, that the unique blending of teacher-psychologist may be realized to the advantage of the pupil.

The purpose of this meeting, then, was to define what the psychologist meant by the "neither here nor there child," to discuss feelings towards these children and to suggest techniques by which such a child might be helped to perform more adequately in school. These children were defined as those whose intelligence falls above the level of the retarded, but below average, or whose intelligence is considerably above average and for whom the particular school system has little in the nature of a special program. In addition, unmotivated and underachieving youngsters were included as not representing the "average" school child, not performing predominantly at the "average" level, that is, at the level expected of them.

The discussion emphasized what was deemed to be a primary

difficulty in working with these children, i.e., lack of the time necessary to divide the class into very small groups for the different subject areas. In addition, teacher–held systems, attitudes, and expectations were discussed. Helping the teachers to recognize what their own feelings often are when faced with a few such seemingly impossible to reach children served as a release for the teachers and as an occasion for the group discussion of techniques that often can work. This led to some very creative thinking concerning these children.

In terms of what the psychologist could offer that was relatively tangible, discussion also involved consideration of developmental patterns at the K–3 age level and how knowledge of these patterns can be tied to a child's interests and experiences as well as his abilities. Specific examples were given involving reading and spelling and the use of games as motivating devices.

VII. Discipline and Teacher Attitudes

The last meeting of the first series of K–3 workshops was concerned with the role of discipline in education and the relationship between discipline and the attitudes held by teachers. Just as there are authoritarian, democratic, and temporizing parents, there are authoritarian, democratic, and temporizing teachers. What creates a particular kind of parent or teacher as this relates to the ruling of the household (or classroom) is obviously a complicated interweaving of a lifetime of experiences and discussion of the backgrounds of such individuals was not the function of this meeting. However, the child is ensnared in many ways by the kind of individual who leads him, and it is the child who is expected to bend flexibly according to the demands of his leaders.

Discipline is a means of control. In early child development it is not expected by the mature adult that the child will sufficiently understand the need for disciplined behavior, that he will effectively discipline himself without the leadership and training provided by adults significant to him. Developmentally, the child responds to the authority of his parents initially because he fears punishment, somewhat later on the developmental scale, because he fears loss of love, still later because he does not like feeling guilty and finally, at a mature level, because he wants to respond in an acceptable way. One step hopefully leads to the next.

Discipline in the classroom serves both as a teaching aid and as teaching matter. As an aid, it helps the teacher establish and maintain limits of acceptable behavior giving the children the security of knowing what is expected of them behaviorally and in this way, it helps the teacher control the class setting. Through the nutrition afforded by fair and consistent discipline, the child is helped to grow to that level when self-discipline becomes increasingly apparent and conceivably, there is less need for discipline to be imposed by others. Just as the child learns to read for the value afforded by reading, so does he recognize the value of self-discipline in everyday living.

The problem of discipline, however, is delineated through the two questions most often raised by teachers: when and how? These were discussed quite fully in terms of a central theme emanating from the teachers' own needs and feelings. Thus, once teachers could discuss the function of discipline, they could also discuss the role of their own expectations regarding this function and why they sometimes disagree about the application of discipline. Here they could see that what disturbed some of them did not disturb others and they could also come to acknowledge that their methods of discipline differed just as well.

At the end of the school year, the teachers in K-3 were sent a questionnaire designed to evaluate the meetings in terms of the teachers' perception of their helpfulness. The questionnaires were responded to anonymously and the responses were overwhelmingly positive. As a result, a second series of meetings was arranged for the following school year and the K-3 series was repeated for the teachers of grades 4-6, with changes made appropriate to the age levels of the pupils.

While it must be remembered that the workshops were not designed to be of therapeutic value to the teachers, certain meetings obviously touched more closely than others on those aspects of human relationships which obviously affect teacher-pupil-parent-psychologist communication. Certain of the meetings were obviously helpful to the teachers in their re-evaluation of themselves in their roles as teachers and in a reappraisal of their expectations of their pupils. Too, the relationship of the teachers to the psychologist changed in many ways, seen both in the change apparent in personal contact and in their attitude toward referral. But, the most obvious change was seen in the type of child referred. No longer was the child with suspected intellectual retardation the predominant referral. Teachers began to refer children who appeared excessively shy and withdrawn--not necessarily the typical acting out child who is such a problem to teachers. And many teachers overtly questioned their own feelings about their relationships with pupils. Apparently, for some teachers at least, the need to be defensive was less obvious, and the general attitude or morale of the teachers seemed to improve. It was as if, in spite of the lack of certain felt needs for remedial teachers and special classes, the teachers felt they had support and guidance not only from the principal, but also from the psychologist.

The workshop series was also a tremendous help to the psychologist. Teachers became individuals who could be identified by name and whose behavior in the classroom could be better understood and more honestly evaluated. They were not just a group of teachers of whom one could be critical, realistically or not. They were individuals, some more able than others, some more flexible than others, but each worthy of consideration on her own merits. Increased respect of these people was one clearly recognizable result as far as the psychologist was concerned and obviously this result was communicated to them with favorable response.

K–3 Workshops: Second Year Program

The second year K–3 workshop series was not designed primarily to be a continuation, in greater detail, of the subjects discussed during the first year. By design, the focus was twofold. It was hoped that topics not discussed at all during the first year might be included to establish a broader base of knowledge regarding child behavior and that certain topics discussed during the first year would be expanded and refined. The psychologist, however, was able to arrange only five meetings for the Fall term, and because of a spring leave of absence, no meetings could be arranged for that time.

Attendance was very good and the interest level of the teachers was quite high. They brought up specific questions regarding certain problem areas, but also discussed rather broad questions for which there were certainly no specific answers. Rapport was excellent and it was obvious that in the give and take of meetings, the teachers and psychologist continued to establish better communication.

I. Deviant Children: The Problems of Being Different.

It was not difficult to discuss the concept of deviation in terms of intellectual, physical and emotional deviation from expected norms. Nor was it difficult to discuss the common causes of deviation, particularly those of environmental origin. Greatest interest, however, was aroused when the most common deviations encountered in the school setting were discussed, and as noted in many of the earlier meetings, the fact that the teachers could readily call to mind concrete examples of the kinds of problems under discussion, added immensely to the meaning of the meeting.

Perhaps, however, of greatest value to the teachers, was the active discussion of what being different means to the child, and of what having a child with some kind of deviation means to the parent. It was apparent that a number of the teachers had never thought about this particular aspect of the problem, but had considered only what it meant to them to have a deviant child in their classrooms.

Certain general rules which the teachers might follow in dealing with deviant children were suggested. In particular, the teachers were encouraged to find out as much as possible from cumulative records, the health office, from the psychologist and principal about the nature of the deviation. They were told that unanswered questions concerning their expectations of the child could possibly be answered or at least honestly discussed and that this might also be discussed with the child directly. The general rule really involved an effort to improve communication and be more sensitive to the child's feelings.

II. Individual Instruction of the Deviant Child.

The purpose of the meeting was not to suggest a bushel full of panaceas for dealing with deviant children but rather to suggest ways in which teachers could work together to create meaningful experiences for their unique pupils, using all their own imaginative skills and knowledge of the mechanics of teaching and of human development.

Altogether too often, teachers rely on the excuse--sometimes valid--that they do not have time to deal with children on an individual basis. It is not simply the inability to find the time during the school day for individual instruction, but teachers do tend to claim they do not have time to devise and create the special techniques the children need. Encouraging group work among teachers is one way in which part of the difficulty may be eliminated. For example, within the framework of teacher–pupil–group cooperation, the psychologist discussed the use of color techniques as aids in improving coordination (writing) skills as well as basic arithmetic concepts and skills. As an example, certain children need concrete aids to learn that multiplication is short–cut addition. Their attention needs to be controlled so that they may see the relationship of addition to multiplication. Color is one way in which this is often accomplished. The child may resent resorting to the "Count the sticks" method, for this may make him feel quite inferior to those children who no longer rely on this method. Teachers working together can set up examples, using colored numbers, to clearly define the steps involved, and with groups of teachers working together, each teacher could rather easily accumulate a set of examples which would then be readily available for use.

Writing skills, in the sense of improved coordination, may be increased through the use of paper with multi-colored lines. The children, themselves, may be able to draw such lines, having the paper available for those youngsters who need it when they need it.

Obviously, through teacher-group cooperation, and the accumulation of short stories children create themselves, it would be possible without the investment of excessive amounts of time, to build a library of reading material based on a combination of word skills available at various reading levels **and** the interest of children at various age and experience levels. In this way, a child unable to read at grade level may be helped to improve his reading skills by use of words at a lower grade level arranged into stories at his interest and experience level.

Each teacher undoubtedly has a storehouse of background in the form of successful and unsuccessful techniques which she has tried with various children. If the teachers can be encouraged to share their particular experiences with each other, there is bound to be an enrichment of experience from which each teacher may draw to stimulate the child deviant for one reason or another. There is no shame in providing "crutches" as learning aids. Individualized instruction does not necessarily have to mean teaching the particular child by himself. The teacher certainly may find considerable assistance all around her, and much of this assistance can come from the child himself.

III. Emotional Development: Stages – Normal and Abnormal.

This was not intended to serve as a course in abnormal psychology, but it was hoped that through a short review of developmental stages, the teachers would become more aware of what is considered relatively normal and abnormal behavior.

Thus, there was discussion of the emotional development of children previous to their entrance into kindergarten. The role of the self-concept was discussed and its relationship to the child's ability to adjust to the demands of a large group situation such as encountered in school, was pointed out. This led rather directly to concern with developmental lag on an emotional basis, as it might be seen in kindergarten and the primary grades.

The point emphasized during the meeting which had considerable "insight" value to the group, was the factor of the interdependency and interaction of emotional maturity with learning. Here emotional readiness was translated into a workable concept integrated with such other educational concepts as experience, motivation, and interest. That a child still uncomfortable in the large group situation might be more concerned with getting the teacher's undivided attention, or his bodily functions, or what his mother is doing with the baby at home, than he is with the primer book in front of him was stressed, as was the reverse situation, where the child is emotionally ready to take those steps leading to his growing emancipation from home.

Finally, certain symptoms of possible developmental lag were reviewed. They included excessive and persistent shyness, nausea, soiling and wetting, repeated attention-getting and acting-out behavior, withdrawal behavior, rocking, sucking, excessive masturbatory activity, temper tantrums, and school phobias. Caution was advised in jumping to diagnostic conclusions, especially since many of these symptoms are transitory in well-adjusted children and here an effort was made to distinguish between "normal" stages and those pointing to abnormality.

IV. Competition: Its Role in Our Social Structure

Obviously, we live in a competitive society. From the intergroup competitiveness of keeping up with the Joneses to the intragroup competitiveness of being bigger and better than one's brother or classmate, competition plays a large role in shaping educational and social values in our society. We are all well aware of the anxiety produced by the cold war nuclear race and we know also the exhorbitant costs in terms of money and comfort. We might well ask if the role of competition as it is manifested in our educational system is one which primarily fosters discomfort or if in any way it may be used to advantage.

Obviously, competition as a special kind of experience, affects behavior. Failure and success experiences leave their mark. They affect the passive child, the aggressive child, the frightened child and the secure child in different ways. They affect drive and they affect levels of aspiration. These experiences also affect self and other evaluation. Since this special kind of experience may prove to be relatively indelible and since it plays a relatively major role in our educational system, it seemed realistic to devote a workshop session to examining competition in terms of its negative and positive features.

As many of us decry the problems of evaluation, many also find it difficult to accept competitiveness as a way of life. We recognize that evaluation of self and others exists and that in spite of its often destructive potentialities, it is a part of our reality. So is competition. Potentially, it may be destructive as well as constructive. Recognizing this duality helps to accept the concept more realistically. Penicillin has been of tremendous value in the treatment of certain diseases. However, there are some people who are allergic to it, and some bacteria which have become resistant to it. It behooves us to be equally aware of the variable effects of competition, healty and unhealthy.

Competition and the urge to compete may have its roots in the need to feel superior. Beating Johnny in the time it takes to solve a multiplication problem helps the winner feel superior to Johnny, regardless of what it does to his appraisal of his ability to do multiplication. At the same time, Johnny's defeat may make him feel inferior to his opponent and possibly in his discomfort, focuses his attention away from the multiplication problem and on to his discomfort.

When we observe that the child comes to school having already experienced jealousy, sibling rivalry, and the like in competing for attention and perhaps for love, above and beyond his desire to have what he believes other children have, he comes to school with a fairly well developed evaluation of his worth, realistic or not. What does the school do when it fosters additional competitiveness?

Competition does provide vigor in the social interaction but this vigor is healthy only if it helps the child discover his limits realistically. This can be effected when the competitors are evenly matched. Do we, however, match our competitors evenly? In spite of such techniques as "homogeneous groups" this is a question that quite probably must be answered in the negative. The loser keeps losing, only a very few people reap the honors since the schools make only a few kinds of awards; honor students compete intensely and often their grades suffer even though they are matched evenly in their homogeneous groups, because the technique of evaluation via grades is too limited. Since the stress is on being the top man, the school that fosters indiscriminate competition creates a setting in which the less–than–top–man is constantly reminded of his inadequacies. Moral surrender, cheating, and cruelty may result. Being a good loser becomes more and more a problem for too many.

As a result of the implications of the above, the workshop centered discussion on the ways in which pupils could derive the benefits of competition using it as a teaching aid. For example, since competitiveness has to be accepted as part of our way of life, team competition may be utilized, especially if the better pupils can be used to give help to the poorer ones as the teams compete. The idea of using the teacher as a pace-setter was also suggested. But perhaps the most valued use can come out of the youngster's learning to compete with himself, setting realistic aspiration levels on the basis of his own self-appraisal as well as the teacher's appraisal of him, for here the rewards in winning become intrinsic. In addition, stressing the strengths and assets inherent in individual differences promotes a realistic awareness of these values as well as a realistic, properly put-in-their-place awareness of weakness. In this way, the likelihood of acceptance of strength and weakness as facts of life to be lived with and worked with is promoted and encouraged.

With the healthy use of competition, its vigor may be gained without the demoralizing side effects.

V. Three R's – Respect, Resignation, and Rejection.

Here the emphasis was placed on the development of respect as a two-dimensional concept, respect for self and respect for others. The attempt was made to draw attention to the relationship of these two aspects of the concept showing how the basis of all respect has to lie in one's ability to respect himself, to trust one's own judgments. With this as something to build on, the teacher can respect the others she must teach, the system in which she works, and the philosophy and goals with which she lives.

The tremendous importance of this concept is clearly seen when we consider what respect does for human relationships. Respect promotes a mutual relationship of honesty between the teacher and her pupil, making blindness in human relations, prejudice and bigotry quite difficult to achieve. While value systems may differ, the person who respects himself is not so defensive that differences become intolerable. Not needing to be defensive about what she stands for, the teacher can be far more objective about the values others hold and the aspirations others have. This provides a positive learning climate, one which motivates all involved to greater understanding of the world in which we live. And not to be disregarded, is the nutritive value to the child of the feeling of "can do" rather than "can't"; with respect, the atmosphere becomes highly conducive to achievement, and the class that is achieving provides further incentive to the teacher and her pupils.

If the respect does not develop in the maturing process, the individual begins to develop a sense of resignation and rejection. Teachers who have little or no self-respect resign themselves in time to an inadequate, unsatisfying, and frustrating career which they must defend to themselves and to others. Pupils exposed to such teachers are unlikely to be positively stimulated. Rather, they are likely to be attacked in one way or another as one of the reasons teaching is so "unsatisfying" and in time, exposed daily to this kind of brainwashing, come to feel as valueless as they have been repeatedly told they are. Children, however, unlike their teachers, cannot resign overtly from the untenable position they hold; they can only resign themselves covertly, coming to class daily with no alternative but to "take it." Enthusiasm disappears and unhealthy, negative attitudes towards school take the place of enthusiasm and positive regard.

Eventually, rejection takes place. It becomes both an active and passive struggle for both teacher and pupil and extends to the community at large. When the educational system of a community is threatened because of a growing lack of respect for it, the very foundations of that community and its growth are threatened. If the rejection that follows is based on a system of criticisms made by people who respect themselves and trust their judgments, the cycle may be broken. But such people become more difficult to find, since they are likely to have been victimized by schools which have rejected them as worthwhile individuals. The vicious circle becomes tighter and more difficult to crack. Inbreeding of this kind is horribly destructive.

With this as the background of the final meeting, a number of remedies of a preventive sort were suggested. The need for self understanding was stressed with special emphasis placed on becoming aware of one's ability to communicate as well as what one communicates. Developing sensitivity to others through conscious effort, making a concerted effort to trust others, to relegate reasonable responsibilities to others as a means of developing trust in one's own judgment and trust in others, were among those suggestions made. Perhaps the most important suggestion, however, was that in our special roles as authority figures we need to recognize what being an authority means to us as individuals, and especially, that it does not mean we cannot err, or that we cannot feel a sense of shame or guilt, or that we cannot be less than perfect and other than human. It does imply, however, that we must be realistic and seek professional counsel when we feel we cannot "make it" on our own.

The workshops were not, nor were they intended to be panaceas. They did, however, bring us closer together and open up many areas of discussion. Communication between teachers and psychologist improved considerably. If they did nothing else, this result made the effort worthwhile.

As noted earlier, they did, however, do something else because the nature of the requests for psychological consultation changed. At this writing, the majority of referrals were concerned not with intellectual deficit or even poor achievement. The concern changed to one involving pupils with behavioral disturbance and not the kind of problems which disrupt the class or which demand disciplinary action. There has been a growing awareness of children who are too shy, too withdrawn, too much the "loners" and there has been a noticeable change of attitude within the faculty regarding the concept of individualized instruction.

This kind of program, successful at Newfane, can certainly be successful elsewhere. It involves compromise in terms of time for neither teacher nor psychologist can be expected to be entirely altruistic. Were released time available, it probably would be easier to gather into the group those teachers who are not really terribly interested in the pupils they teach and, therefore, not too amenable to staying after school without "compensation." Whether an incentive of some kind, extrinsic to what the teacher might gain that would help her as person and teacher, is really crucial to the success of such a workshop program is not easily decided. It does, however, have to be considered carefully. Obviously, we have to accept teachers where they are as well as others, children or adults. Were such a series to be offered again, we would encourage the administration to provide an extrinsic reward, credit towards a salary barrier or compensatory time. The series then would require more than attendance on the part of the teachers and some kind of home study and evaluation would probably be involved.

In a school system with a large faculty, the groups should be no larger than thirty so that discussion can be encouraged. If the meetings are organized to include teachers from many different schools, they should alternate at the different schools. Finally, to gain the benefits of a closer relationship between teachers and psychologists, the meetings should be led by the psychologist serving those teachers. If the psychologist feels he doesn't have the skills or necessary art in leading the workshops, then bringing in another leader would be necessary. The critical consideration, however, lies in the need to keep the meetings concrete with regard to the problems considered and not academic and abstract.

D. Secondary Education Workshops

The proposal of secondary education workshops was predicated upon the experiences of the school psychologist and the curriculum supervisor in analyzing the effectiveness of the elementary education workshops held over a two–year period. The perceptions gained by the authors and the successes achieved by the teacher group therapy at the secondary level indicated that a broad base of general need could be attacked through the planning of a program of secondary education workshops.

These workshops were designed to get at broad understandings and at the same time, specific problems identified through class-room visitation, teacher group therapy, the working of the psychologist with students, and the dealing of the curriculum supervisor in his separate functions with teachers. Such a program, it was hoped, would help develop general awarenesses by teachers which might make them more effective at the junior and senior high school level respectively. The workshops were to include two areas generally involved in curriculum planning and adolescent psychology. It was felt that these could be specifically organized within two separate workshops, one for junior high school teachers and one for senior high school teachers based upon the authors' growing contention that the nature of the educational task with early adolescents in the junior high school must have a focus specifically different from that of the education of later adolescents in the senior high school.

Many of us have long been aware that secondary teachers, whether teaching at the junior high level or the senior high level, in their departmentalized programs have been so subject–centered that they have frequently forgotten the nature of the individuals they teach. Adolescence is a period of very rapid physical growth, of tremendous physiological changes which are and must be reflected by changes of a social and psychological nature. Our contention has been that students will learn far better, far faster, and with greater permanence and transfer if what they learn has meaning to them. The meaning of what a student learns in particular areas of content is bound to be affected by the changes taking place within him. The preadolescent will accept a statement made by an authority because it was made by an authority. Therefore, he doesn't even care about the content of the teacher's statement. A few years later he will challenge such a statement because he rejects authority. If secondary teachers could objectively review the content of the subjects they teach in the light of the changing nature of the students they teach, then the likelihood is that communication will be far more effective.

The point of view held by the secondary teacher is markedly different from that of the elementary teacher because of the nature of the school experience. The elementary teacher is more readily able to understand, through his contact with the atmosphere of the self–contained classroom, the importance of the holistic experience for the youngster. The secondary school teacher is influenced by the disjointedness of the traditional departmentalized approach and tends to be less perceptive of the importance of the holistic approach and thus, is more oriented to the content of his subject matter area which he is likely to teach in isolation from the entire experience of the student. Thus, one of the objectives of the secondary education workshops was to develop an awareness of the importance of the teaching of subject matter in relation to the entire experience of the child.

It will be recalled that the elementary education workshops were primarily planned and led by the psychologist. The focus in that workshop series centered on the recognition and early identification of pupil adjustment problems. This was a second objective in the secondary education workshops, because adjustment problems appear at all levels. While the emphasis on prevention of pupil disturbances implies that efforts be concentrated at the primary and intermediate levels, it would be a serious error to assume that secondary pupils do not run into difficulties of one sort or another that interfere with school behavior and achievement, or that secondary teachers are as aware as they might be of the kinds of problems that do develop only during this age period or of the signs for which they might be looking.

Thus, it can be seen that the objectives of the secondary workshop series were simple. It was hoped that through this in-service approach, teachers would be helped to achieve a greater awareness of the need to teach subject matter in the context of the child's entire experience and not in isolation from it. Secondly, the authors hoped to develop a greater awareness among the teachers of the kinds of problems which secondary pupils often have and in this awareness a sharper sensitivity to these pupils as adolescents.

The authors planned to serve as teachers in the workshop program, working individually within their own specialties, and together in a team endeavor. Each felt more comfortable with certain topics than with others, but in planning the program made provision for considerable exchange.

The following statement of purpose for each of the sixteen sessions was sent to each secondary teacher along with an introductory letter which discussed the mechanics of the proposed workshop and the matter of attendance and tangible rewards. The session starred with a single asterisk was intended for the junior high group, while the double asterisk indicates that session was intended for the senior high group.

Secondary Workshop Outline

I. "And So They Live"

To show by extreme example how the living conditions in a sub-culture can be completely isolated from the objectives of education in that community. This is an attempt to show how completely and absolutely a child's years in school can be unrelated to the rest of his living experience with the result that his education provides him with no means for achieving a better way of life.

II. Teachers' Attitudes and Values – Danger!

To help identify the unrealistic values held by many teachers and to help show how they are imposed upon their students. To indicate how negatively students react to the imposition of these values and how this contributes to the students' blase attitude toward education, school, and teachers.

III. Adolescence: Its General Nature and Sequence (The Struggle for Identity)

To review the nature and development of adolescence as a unique experience of western culture towards the end of the achievement of adult recognition and status. The American school in the great majority of cases does not facilitate this process, but rather frustrates its achievement.

IV. Adolescence: Differences Within and Between the Sexes: The Nature of Defense and the Effects of These on Perception of School and Teachers

To review physical and psychological development within the context of the school. Student behavior does not occur in isolation and the real meaning of student behavior must be understood for effective teaching.

V.* Adolescent Needs: Adjustment to Beginning Adolescence

To help teachers understand the basic problems faced by students at the onset and early stages of adolescence. There is a distinct uniqueness within the early stages of adolescence that must not be confused with the total period we call adolescence. To help teachers become aware of the problems which individual youngsters face if they are either precocious or delayed in the adolescent growth process.

V.** Adolescent Needs: Adjustment to Later Adolescence

To help teachers understand the basic problems faced by students in the later stages of adolescence. It is unrealistic to assume that the older adolescent has the same needs and interests as the junior high school student. To recognize distinctness and overlap is to go a long way towards understanding individual differences.

VI. What is Normal and What Isn't?

To review behavior and its aberrations that the teacher may become a better observer and a more effective participant in the total educational process.

VII.* The Function of the Junior High School: The Task of Education and Its Climate

To help the teacher recognize that since the beginning and early adolescent is a unique individual, the junior high school program must be unique in attempting to develop an educational experience of any real value or meaning. The Junior High School **cannot** be a Senior High School, Jr.

VII.** The Function of the Senior High School: The Task of Education and Its Climate

To help the teacher realize that the senior high school is not isolated subject matter. It must be an experience which will help students become adults and gain a realistic sense of direction as well as educational and vocational skills.

VIII. The Need for Meaning in Learning: Dangers of the Strictly Subject–Centered Approach

To help teachers realize that students will not automatically develop the interest or the degree of interest which each teacher intrinsically has in his 'subject matter. The subject–centered approach with its narrow limits on isolated and highly specialized subject matter is completely remote from the values and interests of the vast majority of students. Learning does not occur in a vacuum.

IX. The Experience–Centered Curriculum

To help teachers realize that learning (the acquisition of attitudes, knowledge, skills, abilities, and the like) is usually, if not always, instrumental to the achievement of some more or less tangible or concrete end or goal. The experience–centered approach has the greatest possibility for organizing subject matter so that students view such subject matter as worth learning and motivating them to learn.

X. Grouping: Its Nature and Purpose

To help teachers realize that grouping is designed to facilitate the students' learning through organizing groups in which they can compete and achieve. Grouping is artificial if it does not allow the student to bring his interests to the level at which he is. Grouping, then, is seen as a catalyst to effective learning.

XI. Remedial Work

To help the teacher realize that remedial learning can take place at all levels, and must take place in the secondary school if the student is to be prepared to take his place in a competitive society with reasonable competency. Without a well–organized developmental program in high school subject areas, no need for an effective remedial program can be identified, nor can one work.

XII. Referral

To help the teacher realize that behavioral deviations occur at **all** levels and that such deviations markedly interfere with the goals of the high school. To help the teacher recognize that learning does not take place by itself. Failure to recognize a student in need of referral can contribute not only to his maladjustment, but to that of the entire learning situation.

XIII. Competition, Test Anxiety, Evaluation, and Discipline

To help teachers realize the impact of these aspects of the classroom situation. Life is replete with competition, anxiety, evaluation, and discipline. These cannot be ignored in the classroom or out of it. Whatever their limitations they serve a purpose. The secondary school purports to help the students live with these realities.

XIV. The Team: Prevention and Cure

To help teachers realize that the classroom is like an athletic field in which working together both behind the scenes and on the forefront is a recognized and essential adjustment to growth. This is crucial for teachers to understand in dealing with students within the educational process as it grows more and more specialized.

XV. Community Criticism of Teachers: What Are Our Defenses, Real and Unreal?

To help teachers admit they are defensive and to ask if those defenses are necessary.

XVI. Responsibilities of the Professional Teacher in the All-School Program

To help the teacher consider what must be done outside of the classroom to earn the respect of the community and the American public. To recognize that the public image he creates must be one respected by the community at-large and educators in particular. Teachers must face themselves.

The foregoing statement was distributed to all faculty and staff and discussed the following day at a faculty meeting at which time certain interesting remarks were made. A number of the teachers viewed the workshop proposed as identical to every course in adolescent psychology which they had ever had in college. It is quite unlikely that this really was valid criticism, but it emphasized the fact that for many teachers the awareness of the interaction between the knowledge that the teacher has of the adolescent in the situation of adolescence and in the situation of school, is quite incomplete. This served to reinforce the conviction held by the authors that much of the knowledge held by teachers of adolescent development is isolated from the reality of adolescent experience within the educational setting.

The following material is the planned presentation of the individual meetings. However, the workshops were not offered because the psychologist author left the situation.

I. "And So They Live" (A Film)

It was felt by the authors that the initial meeting had to achieve more than the orientation expected in a normal course or in-service setting. This film, while fourteen years old, deals with the problem of school children in the Appalachian area in the state of Kentucky. This problem has received increasing national focus through the Anti-Poverty program of the current presidential administration. The film showed the stark poverty and low level of economic achievement for people in this hill country. The realization that this was truly a setting in which education did not serve to enlighten members of the community as to the nature of their problems or how they might go about solving or alleviating them is a stunning one. The complete sterility of the academic materials presented in the school, materials that would never have any practical application for practically the entire population, indicated that curriculum in the schools shown was a dead body of innocuous materials at least fifty years beyond the needs of the people. Materials and data presented were obsolete, inaccurate, extinct but interestingly not resented by the community or the children. Strikingly enough neither the children in this movie nor their families resented the educational process. It was accepted as a way of life. No one, however, raises a question regarding the value of this particular educational process. Conditions of poor health, inadequate housing, farming techniques which were continuing to deplete already barren soils, etc. and the morbidity of outlook make this documentary an especially depressing experience for anyone concerned with human dignity.

It was felt by the authors that this film could direct teachers to the economic extremes in their own school district and community. Through discussion and dramatization the authors hoped to play upon the awe-inspiring impact of this film to communicate the importance of the role of education in helping man to raise himself above a level of bare subsistence. Discussing with the teachers what they would have recommended the school programs do in the Appalachian situation to help these people would lead to a consideration of some of the obviously inadequate areas of the curriculum of their own secondary school which we continue to allow to exist without any critical alarm. The authors were confident that this awareness would remain sufficiently in the minds of all people as to quell any initial reaction of indifference or skepticism regarding the secondary education workshops.

II. Teacher Attitudes and Values – Danger!

The focus in this session was to concern itself with helping the teachers come to an awareness, not only of their own attitudes and their values, but also of the implications of their attitudes and values as these affect and are perceived by the adolescents with whom the teachers deal. Obviously, teachers at the secondary level hold to some degree at least, that the subjects which they teach have value in this presently complex world. The value of these subjects will be defined by the teacher more often than by the pupil. Attitudes held by the teachers will reflect their feelings about not only the subjects which they teach, but about education in general and especially about their perceptions of what people should really be like.

At the same time, it seems advisable to point out to teachers that what they do in their general behavior around the school is observed by their pupils, and while the teachers may consider themselves in isolation as teachers, they are always seen as teachers who happen to be people. Sometimes this peculiar distinction has overtones which are neither understood by the teachers nor by their students.

As long as teachers representing knowledgeable authority figures do not have knowledge of the pupils whom they teach, and as long as they are not aware of the changes that exist from generation to generation, and finally, as long as they do not make themselves aware of the changes in goals and objectives that they themselves held as adolescents and now hold as adults, the communication that exists between these teachers and their pupils will be replete with misunderstanding. What is important to one group of individuals may be considerably less important to a second. How this breach affects the relationship between teacher and pupil was to be the focus of this particular meeting.

The introduction to this session was to be accomplished through role playing. The two authors were very much aware of some of the resistance which the planned workshops had aroused among the faculty members. At the same time the authors were quite convinced that their attitudes concerning the workshops were the only realistic ones; that the workshops did have tremendous value if only the teachers would listen. Thus, the authors decided to assume the role of classroom teacher and impose their own values upon the group before them. This was to be done with no apology and no preparation, but simply a statement of fact that this is important and that is all there is to it. At the end of the session this role playing would have been identified and its purpose explicated in terms of the objectives of the session. Consideration of the effectiveness of the technique in affecting the perception of the secondary teachers was also to have been given.

III. Adolescence: Its General Nature and Sequence (The Struggle for Identity)

Many people admit rather casually that adolescence is a very trying period. They acknowledge that adolescents seem to be neither children nor adults, just big kids with even bigger ideas. People consider that there is or may be a stress and strain in adolescence, but many individuals do not realize either why there is this stress and strain or that this stress and strain can be considerably lightened.

According to one prominent theorist, the struggle for identity is the goal of adolescence and its greatest problem. In his attempt to achieve his identity, the adolescent assumes many different roles simultaneously, some which are easy to cast off and others which are very difficult. He plays this variety of roles even in his school situation. Often there is conflict, not only within his family setting, but within his school setting, for what is permissible and what is urged in the school is not always consistent with the needs of the role the adolescent has chosen to play at that particular time. This contributes to the notion that adolescence is often a period of stress and strain.

One of the most difficult conflicts to resolve for adolescents is the fact that in order to achieve his identity the dependent child has to give up his dependency and assume greater independence of thought and action. The departmentalization process of the American school supposedly heeds and hastens this transition from dependence to independence. In theory, certainly, this is true, but whether it is really true in practice is questionable.

Finally, the American school contributes to a perpetuation of adolescence, a lengthening of the process and a postponement of the transition to adulthood because of the reluctance of many of the American school teachers to relinquish the authoritarian role and to permit the adolescent greater independence of thought and action in spite of the lip service given to it.

This third meeting of the workshops series was to be handled through the lecture and discussion approach. The psychologist author was to present a review of the nature and sequence of adolescent development in terms of the culture in which the adolescent lives. Discussions of the issue were to be defined by key questions and statements emphasizing the educational aspect and contribution to adolescence.

IV. Adolescence: Differences Within and Between the Sexes: The Nature of Defense and the Effects of These on the Perception of School and Teachers

Homogeneity of grouping is a concept most educators are familiar with. Homogeneous groups are established on the basis of chronological age, or education achievement level, or intellectual ability, or perhaps interest in subject matter. Homogeneous groups, however, never really exist in spite of our hopefulness simply because there are so many differences between children that these differences themselves create heterogeneity.

Differences within and between the sexes are often outstanding during adolescence. It is a well known fact that girls reach puberty on the average of two years before their chronological age–mate boys do. Coming to the growth spurt earlier than the boys do, girls in the 5th and 6th grade are often taller than boys and their interests are markedly different from those of boys. Also, there are youngsters who do not begin to reach puberty at the same time that their friends to, some lagging one, two, three, or more years while others are precocious in their development by an equal number of years. Thus, within any so–called homogeneous grouping, differences may be extremely marked not only between the sexes but within the sexes. With the existence of such marked physical and physiological differences, there are also social differences and motivational differences, all of which are bound to affect a child's school relationship.

Student behavior does not occur in isolation and it certainly does not occur in isolation of physical events. Ask any physical education instructor about the increase in excuses among preadolescent and young adolescent girls. That student behavior does not occur in isolation reflects upon the various defensive behaviors of youngsters entering into what is to some degree an unknown future for them. The adolescent who stands out from his peers defends himself for his differences. His need to be defensive because he is uncomfortable in his strangeness affects his perception, not only of his peers but also of his school and of his teachers.

The psychologist author was to approach this meeting via the lecture route with pertinent questions designed to lead into general discussion. In particular it was hoped that the teachers would raise questions reflecting their own concern in their own perception of the teen–ager who becomes a physiological adolescent relatively late or of the not–yet teen–ager who becomes a physiological adolescent too early.

V.* Adolescent Needs: Adjustment to Beginning Adolescence

The junior high school has purportedly evolved to meet the "educational needs of the early adolescent." Until relatively recently, the area of psychology has not spelled out the specific characteristics or the several needs of the early adolescent as opposed to the later adolescent. Rather it has treated adolescence as a singular unit of growth psychologically. At the time the junior high school was developed at the turn of this century, the foremost expert in adolescent psychology, G. Stanley Hall, carefully defined adolescence as a singular unit of growth. While psychology and education have alluded to these mythical areas of early adolescence as opposed to later adolescence, little has been done to identify and specify the important differences between these two aspects of adolescence. Failure of the junior high school in many instances to be succinctly effective has stemmed from the fact that the observable differences which people can identify between the junior and senior high school student are not reflected in the orientation of junior high school and senior high school teachers. Thus, the junior high school in considering adolescence as a singular unit of growth, generalizes and does not organize its program and approach toward meeting the real needs of the typical junior high school student who may be as described earlier, either approaching pubescence, achieving it, or still a year or two from achieving it. The concomitant of this situation means that the generalized approach of the junior high school, will in most cases quite consistently miss the mark psychologically for most of its students. Thus, the objective of this particular program for junior high school teachers or for teachers who teach both junior and senior high school classes, was to spell out in operational setting, those differences about junior high school students and how they should be considered in the planning, organization, and implementation of the junior high school instructional and all-school program. The realization to be gained by teachers was that failure to continue to organize junior high school instructional practices which were at odds with the needs and the capabilities of the junior high school early adolescent, would be a commitment to maintaining and extending curricular experiences which could not be perceived by the junior high school as important and which could not hope to help the junior high school student solve problems he faced at that time or be prepared to approach the problems of later adolescence and the demands of the senior high school.

One of the most obvious adjustments which the young adolescent must make is that involving an understanding of the physiological changes taking place within his body. Many parents have observed changes in moods which they have felt were inexplicable on an environmental basis. Many educators assume that parents and teachers have joined together to educate the young adolescent boy and girl about their bodily changes and what these mean. Such changes may be understood intellectually or they may not. What many of us have neglected, however, is the fact that these intellectual understandings are paralleled by attitudes which also need to be understood. Unfortunately many of us have neglected to incorporate in Health and in Physical Education classes those kinds of understandings which children must realistically accept without emotional upheaval. The big struggle in early adolescence is essentially the physical one. With it too, for the first time there occurs a change in moral consideration. The student is not simply concerned with whether he should cheat or not, steal or not, but he is also concerned for the first time with an awareness of sex urges.

Knowing what we already do concerning the differences within and between the sexes as these apply at early adolescence, we need to ask ourselves just what the junior high school has set out to accomplish and to reflect upon the too well established habits of 7th grade dances and the like, the justification of which is not clear.

V.** Adolescent Needs: Adjustment to Later Adolescence

Later adolescence bears little resemblance to early adolescence. Physical adjustments have in general been made. The end of one's public school education is approached. Vocational choices and choices with regard to further education are no longer abstract concepts which can be decided tomorrow, but are concepts which the adolescent now faces knowing that he is about to embark on a plan of life. He has played many roles, kept some, and discarded others. More and more he is expected to behave like the adult he now physically resembles, and more and more he demands to be treated like an adult. His growth towards greater independence and his nearness to the achievement of identity have moved him much closer to the end results of the adolescent transition than he was at the beginning.

However, the senior high school does not develop its operational pattern to coincide with this development in the adolescent. In 12th grade the adolescent is one year away from being an independent, self–directive, self–supporting adult when he will enter the world of work and society at–large. Logically, it would seem that the total scope of junior and senior high school education should develop a pattern of activities which offer increasing opportunity for adolescents to be more responsible and independently self–directive as they develop such capacities. Unfortunately, a 12th grade student has practically no more opportunity to develop such individual responsibility and to experience the fulfillment of such responsibility than does the 7th grade student. This is bound to mean that many 12th grade students, although they would have the capacity for such self–direction, are completely frustrated and in a sense largely unprepared to handle the complete responsibility which adult citizenship will suddenly impose upon them immediately upon leaving school. Such preparation is not realistic in that the older adolescent has not had the opportunity to gradually progress in his skills in operating independently. Thus, in this respect the regimen of the senior high school is detrimental to the development of individual responsibility for many later adolescents. Rather by moving completely under an authoritarian directive system which stresses conformity to a conditioned response in terms of bell schedules, and other institutionalized practices, the later adolescent is definitely hindered from developing sophistication or operational attitudes which he will need when called upon to make critical decisions as a young adult facing the responsibilities that will soon be thrust upon him.

This program, similar to the one for junior high school adolescent needs, was to be handled through a rather succinct lecture designed to stimulate arousal and discussion of key points which could be made within the interaction of group discussion.

VI. What is Normal and What Isn't?

Although the purpose of this particular meeting was to review behavioral aberrations, it also seemed advisable to discuss the meaning of the term normal which is so freely used. Much of what is said is perceived differently by different people in the framework of their own background of experiences. The term normal or what is often considered its equivalent, average, has different meaning not only to different people, but also in regard to different things. Thus, the child with average intelligence may be perceived by his teacher as a dull child if she is teaching bright children, may be perceived by his parents as a happy child, or may be perceived by his parents as a terribly disappointing child with no future. The concept average applied to one's physical development is generally received quite differently than the concept average applied to intelligence. The letter grade C which supposedly means average is received differently, depending upon what the grade before was, i.e., whether it was a D or a B.

Within this framework of the differing interpretations given to the terms normal and average, the focus of the meeting was to be turned to an understanding of what is reasonably normal behavior for adolescents of the age level under consideration. This meeting was to be handled on an orientation basis rather than a lecture and discussion basis. Dittoed statements were prepared to be distributed to teachers identifying specific behavior categories with general statements as to manifestations of the problems. These were to be generally discussed.

VII.* The Function of the Junior High School: The Task of Education and Its Climate

This meeting was specifically designed to follow the meeting identifying the educational needs of early adolescents. Ditto statements on the role and function of the junior high school and its critical objective of articulating the elementary and senior high school system were to be presented to teachers previous to the meetings. Discussion was to be predicated upon their reading this material. The identification of skills necessary at this level to help youngsters begin to move toward possible selections for academic preparation in the high school as opposed to vocational definition were to be identified as important functions of the junior high school.

The role of general education as opposed to special education and beginning the preparation for and involvement in special education are put forth as awarenesses which most junior high school teachers do not possess, and as areas in which the junior high school begins to become frustrating for students. Specific grade level planning and consideration of a realistic expectation of attention and interest spans were to be identified as well as the ramifications of these for the classroom teacher. The focus upon particular teachers' roles as representing either general education, exploratory, or special education were to be identified and the importance for coordination among these three areas was to be stressed. The importance of the adjustment process critically necessary for the junior high school was to be another realization which this meeting sought to achieve. Ramifications were noted for junior high school and elementary school guidance people and general faculty in the preparation of these youngsters to move in a secure and realistic fashion from the atmosphere of the self-contained elementary school classroom to the beginnings of departmentalization in the junior high school. Dittoed materials designed to identify points of departure for discussion by curriculum groups were to be distributed.

VII.** The Function of the Senior High School: The Task of Education and Its Climate

This meeting was to be designed for senior high school teachers as well as those who share teaching responsibility in junior and senior high school grades. Specific considerations of the role and function of the senior high school as a culminating process in the American public school system and the role of this institution as either terminal or preparatory for further education were to be prepared in a dittoed bulletin and submitted to teachers the week before the meeting to be read and discussed at this meeting. Discussion was to be developed by initial questions from the curriculum supervisor after a brief initial comment stating some specific problems which the senior high school has not been successful in solving or alleviating. From the comments of the group, reference to the points in the dittoed bulletin as well as supplementary material prepared by the supervisor were to be interrelated. The importance of providing a comprehensive high school program with equal consideration to the problems of the student going on to further education, the nature of what this education should be, and similar consideration of the student going on to vocational preparation, or the student with no defined goal beyond high school is a point of failure which continues to be a dilemma in the operational American senior high school. Particular identification of the role of subject matter and how this subject matter should help students to gain skills, facts, and information, as well as attitudinal approach so that the subject matter taught by the school will be perceived as worth learning by the senior high school student was to be discussed. In approaching this learning experience, though, the student must have developed or be in the process of developing a point of view for his own continuum beyond the experience of the high school. Failure for this to develop in the first place or for this failure to be compounded by lack of perception of why subject matter should be learned, is another monumental task with which the high school has never come firmly to grips.

Some consideration preparatory to the meetings scheduled as VIII and IX were to be prepared in a brief study of the nature of learning and how it takes place. This was designed to help teachers consider what the nature of learning should be and to show the degree to which the American high school structures learning by rote. The senior high school must be concerned with developing a climate for learning within an experiential and functional context and to decide what the climate should be that would best facilitate this.

Students of middle class orientation having average or above-average ability develop values which ascribe to the importance of education. This may be education either as preparation for further education or for specific vocational orientation. Students having something less than this unfortunately have not found the senior high school organized to the point of helping them find such values as these and others in preparation for their entering the world of adult society as individuals ready to undertake an understanding participation in a democratic society.

VIII. The Need for Meaning in Learning: Dangers of the Strictly Subject-Centered Approach

This meeting was planned to help teachers graphically see how dangerous the strictly subject-centered approach is to teaching. The secondary school in the senior high school program has a heavy emphasis upon the teaching of subject matter and in the areas of special education can be expected to be heavily subject-centered. The subject-centered approach can be quite effective in senior high school special education areas because of student interest or their select abilities. Either of these two qualifications develop a high degree of homogeniety. However, in the general education areas of the senior high school where such selectivity is not to be found, and in the junior high school, which is basically a general education institution, the subject-centered approach is least justifiable and cannot be honestly predicted to develop learning which will be anything more than rote learning to be regurgitated on pencil and paper tests and then forgotten in ever-increasing amounts. This session was to be conducted with discussion of materials distributed two weeks before the meeting for study by the group.

The subject-centered approach quite often encourages the teacher to plan his courses based heavily upon his intrinsic interests in his own subject-matter area assuming that such interests can be generated in the minds of students. The subject-centered approach is likely to be quite remote from the immediate felt needs and the problems of adolescents. Likewise, the necessarily limited scope in the pre-organized sequence of this approach makes it most difficult to adequately meet individual differences among students. In this approach the "subject matter for subject matter's sake" directs the mastery of subject-matter to become the principal goal of the learning situation. It does not seek the cultivation of knowledge as it must be related to the world around us in an atmosphere and environment which the student can understand and in which he has an interest. This is not to imply that the subject-centered approach is all negative. It is rather that the usual implementation of the subject-centered approach tends to place almost all emphasis upon the subject matter and not upon learning it for some real purposes other than the mere mastery of content.

On the positive side, it must be recognized that the subject-centered approach toward learning has the support of tradition and is generally approved by teachers, parents, and students. Since the subject-centered curriculum is in use almost universally in high schools, colleges, and universities, it follows that teachers, parents, and students are products of this system of education and through conditioning come to feel comfortable with it. The organization of the subject-centered approach is simple and easily understood and it lends itself to the preparation and use of textbooks which have always been the backbone of instructional materials. The subject–centered curriculum is easily changed and kept up–to–date since most schools "revise" curriculum by rearranging the blocks (units or subjects), by adding or dropping subjects and by adopting new textbooks. This "broken–front" concept of curriculum development lends itself to the examination and change of aspects of the curriculum without much thought given to general program development.

The wide range of socio–economic population and the manifold interests and problems brought to the American public secondary school cannot be truly effectively handled by the subject–centered approach to curriculum planning and the organization of learning. This meeting was to direct teacher focus to realize that the course of social change in America renders the subject–centered approach effective only in upper–middle class situations as well as in the more highly selective facets of special education as it is offered within the senior high school. Even within these situations there are other forms of curricular organization which have a greater predictability for success in terms of developing effective learning situations than the subject–centered approach.

IX. The Experience–Centered Curriculum

This session was planned to help teachers understand by definition and practice what the experience–centered approach to curriculum planning is as well as to develop a basic framework of how it could become operational within their own junior and senior high school programs.

This session was to be predicated upon the distribution of materials two weeks before which would require reading and interpretation. Emphasis was to be upon the consideration of what aspects of an approach to learning should be best understood by students as well as teachers. Acceptance of the experience–centered approach to curriculum planning and learning is predicated upon the assumption that effective learning is most often, if not universally, directed toward the achievement of some more–or–less tangible or concrete goal of the learner. The experience–centered approach develops upon the present experience of the student and his problems and interests take on an important role in determining appropriate activities in planning, implementing and evaluating learning situations. Initially, it should be made clear that all activities, whether they be experience – or subject–matter–centered, are most effective when the foregoing principle is considered. However, when the very nature of the activity depends upon its close interaction with the contemporary life experience of the student, this principle takes on new meaning. Extrinsic motivation in a Mathematics class may be gradually transformed into a wholehearted interest in due time, but the direct–experience activity is doomed to failure from the start if the student is not activated by a strong motive for carrying it onward.

The sequence of learning activities in the experience–centered approach is determined by maturational levels, integration of personality, growth processes, and the extension of problems and interests rather than the internal logic of a field of knowledge, as would apply in the subject–centered approach. In contrast with subject–centered activities having an "in–built" scope and sequence pattern, the experience–centered approach reverses such a situation because of the environment, stress and strain in a particular situation and the definable problems of the students. Thus, in the experience–centered approach, the student's growth and development become the central factors in determining what to do next. This does not mean that the student does whatever he wants to do, but rather that the intelligent teacher, looking at the student in terms of all the factors which are affecting the student in his present life, his hopes and his personal aspirations, becomes a partner with him in planning a sequence of his classroom learning experience. One unit of experience leads into another as new environmental conditions evolve and claim recognition. The determination of sequence becomes a more flexible situation which cannot be categorized in terms of "so much ground **will** be covered during the month of September."

This session, through description of specific situations and discussion, was planned to help teachers to identify the strengths and weaknesses as well as the difficulties to be encountered in the experience–centered approach. Toward this direction, it must be realized that facts and principles of subject matter are often learned in a matrix of direct experience which are not always permanently retained or transferred to new situations. To this end, teachers in the experienced–centered approach must teach for transfer.

Teachers are not readily prepared in large numbers to carry on the experience–centered approach so that in–service education experiences would be necessary. The acceptance of this approach would necessitate a reconsideration of curriculum planning in the school which would have to depart from the "broken–front" concept of curriculum development. Successful development of experience–centered programs and curricula on a school–wide basis cannot be undertaken unless considerable thought is given to general program development in the total scope and sequence of the total curriculum of the school. At the same time, it must be recognized by teachers that experience–centered programs do not always make adequate provision for logical organization. Many of the proponents of this experience-centered approach to learning are to be blamed for this criticism. They deserve it. When the logical organization of subjects, with its easily understood scope and sequences is abandoned, all too frequently logical organization is thrown completely out. Failure to develop an adequate frame of reference which will provide sound principles for determining scope and sequence will certainly doom the experience-centered curriculum as opportunistic and ineffective.

Specific emphasis was to be placed upon helping teachers identify the advantages to be gained in an experience-centered approach. Acceptance of this approach also predicates acceptance that the personal experience centered activities must be closely related to the needs, problems, and interests of the student. It would follow that a school would wish to break with the complete emphasis upon "logically" organized subject matter as a basis for the curriculum if it were seeking to plan its program in terms of natural, first-hand personal experience. The experience-centered approach seeks to utilize to the fullest extent the environment, both physical and social, of the school and community, and thus possesses a very real potential for unifying the school and the community. The experience-centered approach is easily oriented to the development of democratic values dramatically beyond what the subject-centered approach could do, and can promote the unification of various aspects of school living during the school day.

The strongest recommendation for the experience-centered approach is that it is consistent with the organismic psychology of learning. Learning is an active process and it takes place most effectively when the organism faces real problems requiring the use of intelligence for their solution. The experience-centered approach provides an excellent setting for this type of learning. The facing of situations which are an integral part of the student's changing environment are the best guarantee of transfer of training to other situations. If the teacher has been made alert to the possibilities for this transfer, the unified nature of the activities which can be developed through the experience-centered approach, can stimulate the process of integration in the growth of the student which the subject-centered approach cannot accomplish and can only hope to achieve through coincidence.

X. Grouping: Its Nature and Purpose

Individuals with the same interests, with the same income level, individuals with the same or similar religious backgrounds, get together and form their own groups. This is perhaps a "natural" form of grouping. It provides for a certain level of similarity which is supposed to make relationships easier.

Grouping in the school situation is effective if it is catalytic to effective learning. The group is created to provide meaningful competition, similarity of achievement and experience background so that growth is possible for all, and to provide a chance for all to experience a new interest in learning. Actually, it is hoped that the student who has experienced much failure and much disinterest will have a chance finally to achieve success and become interested. It is hoped that the student who is always at the bottom of his group will now stand a chance to be in the middle or at the top on the basis of his own strengths.

Grouping is no panacea. It does not really make teaching easier, but it may make it far more effective. In providing the student an opportunity to work successfully in a situation which is competitive, like the world in which the student must live and adults must work, the student has an opportunity to achieve success in competition with a group whose range of abilities and interests in the given subject matter area will constitute a fair range of challenge. For the organization of instruction, grouping may provide a more realistic focus of trying to meet succinct educational objectives in specific categories in which there is a somewhat tighter range of interests and abilities. Information to be communicated and learned may be more realistically and understandably organized and communication can be confined to a more succinct level. This avoids the problems of communication raised in situations in which the teacher has to reach students whose backgrounds vary widely and whose abilities and interests fall into a wide range of difference. Grouping should also be utilized to develop curricular experiences of breadth, depth, and specific ranges of interest.

Unfortunately, many teachers expect that once grouping is developed the range within a class is so narrow that they do not have to worry about grouping within that class. This is a naive assumption. There has to be a range with a given group even though the distribution may be skewed. Teachers approaching a relatively tight program of grouping often forget that no matter how tight the grouping, the class still is composed of individuals with their own interests, abilities, and personalities. They are still a group of individuals with a range of abilities, skills, and perceptions which must be considered so that small group and individualized instruction will properly remain a part of the classroom setting. No matter how tight the group, there will always be those fringe students who are to be borderline, not quite a part of the group or apart from it.

Grouping is artificial if it does not allow the student to bring his interests to his level of ability. This means that while a student may be grouped in a below-average situation in certain areas of study, it is not at all unreasonable that in other areas of study he will be at an average level or perhaps even higher. It should be remembered that this is quite likely to be the case in situations involving abstract versus non-abstract kinds of learnings.

This meeting was to be handled around dittoed materials which were to be distributed to members of the group a week before the meeting and read for consideration, discussion, and further development in the meeting.

XI. Remedial Work

The key understanding to be arrived at by teachers with regard to this meeting was that remedial work is far too often seen as a panacea to make up for lack of learning or lack of effective teaching. This it can never be. Remedial work can never be realistically planned or instituted in any aspect of the secondary school unless there is first the development of a realistic and broad developmental program in that particular area. Once the developmental program has been organized and implemented, the student who has fallen behind or who has the lack of ability to learn at a certain level, may be helped on a remedial basis to be brought back to the level at which he should be. If the developmental program is adequate to the needs of the student, the student will then be able to pick up and grow with his peers although some additional or concurrent remedial help may be necessary. To offer remedial services apart from a developmental program will mean that the student is merely brought to a specific ability level and then put into a regular class setting. At this time he is likely not to progress again and the remedial approach will then have to be used as a ladder to get him to the desired rung. Adequate scope and sequence must be formulated in the institution of such a developmental program to identify what the remedial service should be, to what extent it should be operational and how it should be implemented.

An instance of a critical need for a developmental program is in the area of reading. Reading is taught directly in the primary grades and supposedly in the intermediate grades and then, incidentally, is part of the English Language-Arts curriculum in grades 7 through 12. For the youngster having difficulty in reading, isolated remedial services in the junior or senior high school program will only bring him back to a certain point, and if there is no well thought out and operating developmental program of reading, the youngster will not be in a setting in which he can be expected to grow and develop in a planned, sequential fashion. Remedial services in a program such as reading can be adequate if the nature of the development program is sufficiently defined so that remedial needs for specific individuals not achieving within the normal program can be readily identified and a remedial plan for individuals or for a group of individuals planned and operationalized. Sequential development following on the basis of experience, ability, and interest is essential.

At the same time, it is hoped that teachers realize the importance and need for remedial approaches within existing programs as they are developmental. Quite often a remedial program will not be considered because teachers feel the condition, in terms of a particular program or particular students, is irreparable.

It is never too late to begin a program of remediation. In spite of well known literature which suggests that remedial reading, for example, begun in the secondary school years is very ineffective, the authors question whether remediation must always be ineffective even if it is begun for the first time at the secondary school level. If remedial work is incorporated in a developmental program which takes cognizance of not only the individual's ability but of his interest and motivation, and which helps the individual student recognize what needs he might have for skills which he has let go by the board, it is quite possible that such remedial work will indeed be effective. It is not an unknown finding that drop-outs and people who have long since left school have returned to academic settings and made rapid progress in areas in which they were extremely deficient previously. The suggestion, here, is that remedial work will be as successful as the recognition of interests and developmental level permits.

This meeting was to be handled through lecture and discussion. Approaches to remedial programs which had been developed within the Newfane secondary school setting and areas which might be worth considering for the development of remedial programs at the present time were to be discussed in some detail.

XII. Referral

Using lecture technique and simulation technique, the purpose and nature of referral to the psychologist was to be discussed.

Specifically, it is important to emphasize that the purpose of a psychological referral is multiple. Certainly, the referral is made to help the child and this is the primary function, but helping the child is only one of the reasons for referring him. A child who is not responding well in the classroom regardless of the reasons, is a disturbing influence to any perceptive teacher.

A youngster is referred to the psychologist because something is wrong. It matters considerably in terms of the diagnosis and prognosis what is wrong with the child, but unless someone close to the child makes the perception that there is something wrong, no help can be offered.

There are eight areas which the psychologist considers worthy of discussion as representative of the kinds of problems which teachers at any level may meet. These include learning problems, behavioral problems, problems involving peer and authority relationships, school truancy, achievement deficiencies, certain types of physical problems, withdrawal problems, and school phobias. The latter problem is not likely to be at all common at the secondary level but when it occurs it is truly a source for concern.

Two sample case studies follow and these were to be used as simulation items to introduce this particular session:

1. John S. has a record of academic excellence. He has always maintained superior achievement level but has never contributed to classroom discussion unless questions are directed at him specifically. John is extremely quiet, and is rarely seen to enter or leave a classroom with a boy or a girl. He has never been seen at extra–school functions.

John, a 9th grader, has recently begun to appear more and more uncomfortable in the presence of his classmates. His homework in English and Social Studies has deteriorated.

Physically, John presents a relatively awkward appearance. He is considerably taller than most of his male classmates. His complexion is extremely poor and his voice is quite uncontrollable. The Phys. Ed. teacher indicates that John has complained about taking showers after gym, and recently has reported on a number of occasions to the nurse just before gym claiming illness.

2. Paul R. has always been a marginal student. He was placed in the 7th grade slow group because of poor achievement. He is slightly built, shows no signs of puberty, and recently his disinterest in school has become more and more apparent. He continues to behave as if he can hardly wait to quit school.

Group intelligence tests indicate that Paul has an I.Q. of 88. He has two older brothers, neither of whom completed high school. His parents have not been very cooperative as far as attendance at school functions or teacher conferences are concerned.

Paul claims that as a "retard" he cannot perform in school. He also claims there is no need for him to learn any skills because he will be taken care of by the welfare as long as he needs help.

After class discussion concerning these cases, the psychologist was to discuss the kinds of things which the secondary school teacher could be expected to observe in the departmentalized setting regarding any particular student. After this, the psychologist was to discuss with the group what the nature of the psychological evaluation is and what might be expected to follow after the evaluation has been completed.

XIII. Competition, Test–Anxiety, Evaluation, and Discipline

In order to create an impact in this meeting such as teachers often create unknowingly in their own classrooms, the teachers were to be given a test involving digit–symbol associations which they will have to commit to memory in order to be able to do arithmetic problems of increasing difficulty. The teachers were to be told that this is a new test of intelligence involving teachers' ability to learn something to which they have not been previously exposed and to apply this learning in a power–test situation. The test was to take approximately ten minutes.

After collecting the papers and presenting the correct answers to the test questions, the discussion leaders were then to ask the teachers what they felt about the nature of the test, the expectations of the discussion leaders concerning the teachers, and whether the test was truly fair. Because of the nature of the test, this should lead to discussion of evaluation and anxiety around test–taking activities. Because of the nature of the test, also, the element of competition should be brought out and a statement made about the effect of competitiveness as this is related to test–taking activities.

The nature of test–anxiety was then to be discussed in terms of its influence on defensive behavior, learning, and as a drive. Once the teachers came to an awareness of the role of test–anxiety, the hoax to which they were exposed was to be explained. The perspective which the teachers should have gained concerning their own feelings of a few minutes ago should lead to a discussion of competitiveness among secondary students and the effect of competitiveness on evaluation and discipline. This was all to be done as lecture–discussion.

XIV. The Team: Prevention and Cure

This session was to be introduced by the use of a simulation technique and followed by discussion with some direct lecture presentation. Primary emphasis was to be directed toward showing the teachers the difficulties and lack of communication which can result in a school setting where there is complete lack of the team approach with the isolation of teachers, departments, grade levels, and special services of the school. Primary emphasis here was to be upon helping teachers to see where their knowledge about students, instructional problems, and subject matter can best be shared for greater effectiveness within the all-school program. The role of special services, particularly pupil personnel services, was to be identified in terms of the coordinating function such services provide for teachers by organizing the instructional program and bringing teachers together to discuss common problems as well as problems regarding particular students or problems of a grade level nature. Even the most excellent teacher cannot achieve optimum results if he operates in a situation of isolation in which the classroom becomes his impenetrable kingdom. This is also true of the teacher who resents inquiry by other teachers or school personnel and considers such inquiry and observation as unwelcome and unnecessary interference. The following simulation technique was to be discussed at the beginning of the class.

Miss Brown is a beginning 9th grade English teacher at East Nowhere Central School. Her classes have been heterogeneously grouped and the only information she was given at the beginning of the school year was class lists from the guidance office with no particular commentaries as to extremely able or slow students in her heterogeneous classes. Mrs. Smith, a veteran English teacher, whose room is next to Miss Brown's prides herself on her skills but hesitates to share any of her successful experiences with other teachers. She contends teachers should be able to develop their own approaches rather than borrow or steal techniques which have been worked on in great detail and with some difficulty by other teachers. Miss Brown's initial questions to Mrs. Smith were rebuffed with, "Don't worry, you'll learn like we all did." While some discipline problems have begun to show in her classroom, Miss Brown is hesitant to approach the administrator who stated in faculty meetings that teachers should be able to control their own situations and not wantonly send students with trifling problems down to the office. The school's guidance counselor also has the duties of assistant principal in addition to full-time scheduling and has indicated that early in the year he does not wish to be bothered with teacher problems, suggesting that they should work things out among themselves.

What do you see as the alternative for Miss Brown in her situation and how would you suggest that she go about gaining information about the students in her class or help for the critical situations which may be developing?

XV. Community Criticism of Teachers: What Are Our Defenses, Real and Unreal?

Excerpts of statements made in the local press, statements made by well-known writers critical of education, parent comments about the length of the teachers' day, and extensive summer vacations were to be dittoed and passed out to each of the teachers in the group. Their reactions were to be solicited and notes taken concerning their comments. These comments were then to be discussed in terms of teacher defensiveness and whether the defensiveness is warranted or not.

The concept of professionalism and teaching as a profession were then to be raised. The purpose in raising this as an issue for discussion relates to the concept as one in which there are considerable contradictions in terms of expectation and performance.

The teachers were to be asked to submit a short paragraph in which they were to describe the motivations they had for becoming teachers and whether they felt their motives had been met. It was expected that the answers would show evidence that many of them have little or no awareness of their motivations in entering teaching and that many of them would be quite dissatisfied with what they have gained from teaching as a profession. This was to be related to the defensiveness which teachers have.

A final point to be raised was to involve the extent of the differences existing between the expectations which teachers have of themselves and the expectations that teachers feel members of the community have of them. This difference is expected to be quite large and should lead to a clarification of the issues around whether their expectations are reality-oriented.

The primary purpose of this meeting was to help teachers admit that they are defensive and to help them ask of themselves if it is necessary for them to be so defensive. If it is necessary for them to be defensive, then they must consider the need to take a closer look at themselves, a look that is more honest.

XVI. Responsibilities of the Professional Teacher in the All-School Program

The public image of the public school teacher varies between extremes of respect for the teacher as a paragon of virtue and knowledge and the extreme of dismay that the teacher is a disseminator of peculiar and often incorrect knowledge. Whatever the teacher really is, in the public eye and in truth, he has a position of considerable responsibility. Teachers represent a group of people with a minimum of a four-year college education and with a value system which perpetuates education.

Using lecture and discussion technique, this meeting was to attempt to raise the question of the responsibilities of the professional teacher, not only in the school in which she teaches, but in the community in which she lives. Some of the responsibilities which were to be raised for discussion include:

1. The teacher's behavior in the local bar.
2. The teacher and the second job.
3. The teacher taking an active role to improve the status of his profession.
4. The teacher as a church member.
5. The teacher as a non-church member.
6. The teacher as student in graduate courses.
7. The teacher as scout leader.

In all these positions, the teacher projects an image. Just as the physician has come to assume a more realistic place in our present society, the teacher must yet find his place in our present society and must educate the non-teacher to an acceptance of him as a shade of grey between the extremes.

The research paper which was to be required of each participant in both groups focuses upon the application of aspects of the in-service program as related to the teacher's teaching assignment with regard to his subject-matter area and/or grade level. The paper should be analytic to describing some of the problems attacked in the in-service experience as they are present in the teacher's program and then describe how the teacher would plan to alleviate these conditions in terms of some of the positive approaches suggested during the in-service experience. This might, in some instances, lead to the development of a new course outline for the programs taught by teachers themselves.

In addition, teachers were to be required to construct two tests. The first is to represent a test based upon the teacher's subject area with instructions designed to increase student anxiety. The second will be a test also based upon the teacher's subject area, but with instructions so designed to eliminate or alleviate test-anxiety.

The teachers were also to be required to create a competitive situation in which the students who are achieving least well in the classroom will be helped to successful experience. The experience will be one applicable with relative ease to the teacher's own classroom situation.

It is hoped that in having the teachers write a research paper, developing the tests and creating the competitive situation, that the authors will be able to evaluate whether or not the teachers truly gained an understanding of the concepts being presented. This will be used by the discussion leaders in modifying their own roles in the series of meetings for future presentations.

E. Unit Planning

The cooperative interactions of the two authors at the secondary school level allowed the school psychologist to be brought into the planning of curriculum. This was done after the psychologist had visited classes by invitation and as the result of follow-up conferences with the teachers involved. In such conference settings teachers became aware of the desire of the authors to develop a preventive rather than the traditional diagnostic and therapeutic approach in working with the problems of students who were having difficulty adjusting to curricula and the all-school program as it had been developed. These conferences helped teachers develop an enthusiasm for the idea of planning a curriculum which would facilitate the alleviation and obviation of some of these problems as the psychologist had become aware of them in working with students and the guidance counsellors.

In working with the curriculum specialist and teachers, the psychologist was able to identify areas of problem and misunderstanding experienced by students toward which existing curricular areas and programs had contributed. The planning of units was begun in those subject-matter areas represented by the teachers whose classes were visited by the two authors based on the follow-up conferences just described. Four units were planned in this fashion and enthusiastically received by teachers involved in the planning with the authors and were implemented in the secondary school program.

While many units were being sketched for such planning in a wide range of subject matter areas, the departure of the psychologist author from the school setting meant that only four units were actually carried through the planning and implementation procedures described. The four units are: (1) "Nutrition and Vitamin Deficiency, a Unit for Ninth Grade General Science;" (2) "Tobacco, Alcohol, and Narcotics, Three Sub-Units for Seventh Grade Health;" (3) "The Study of Nutrition and Its Relation to Culture and Society, a Unit for Ninth Grade Core classes or for formal correlation in English Language-Arts, Social Studies and Health;" and (4) "Democracy - How It Affects People, a Unit for World History." It is felt that these units have broad possibilities for implementation in most schools and can be adapted to the instructional materials already in use. For this reason only brief reference is made in these units to specific instructional materials and in most instances these are suggestions for introductory activities for the units. In other instances, as in the World History Unit, no such materials are suggested since any current World History text will suffice.

The focal point in these units is their attempt to organize activities around ideas and points of interest which it is felt are meaningful and of real interest to students. The activities are designed to help relate the curricular experiences to the curiosities and interests of the students beyond the apathetic approach which students have indicated they take toward the curricular areas which these units represent. The experience of planning the units helped teachers to develop awareness of the apathy which students have usually brought to the unit areas.

In their initial implementation, each of the four units helped students to develop a significantly greater amount of interest in the content covered by the units than in the previous experiences of the teachers. This served to boost even the initial enthusiasm of teachers shown in the planning sessions with the authors and they looked forward to planning more and different units. Student interest and achievement during the units was higher and in semester and final examinations their retention of information and organization of it and the expected understandings was much more effective than in other units of the courses.

Although the psychologist author left the school, there was considerable carry over among the teachers who had been involved in these unit planning experiences. Their planning of units with the curriculum specialist retained the perceptions and awarenesses of the importance of gearing units to hit real interests of students as much as possible. These teachers in turn have had some further influence in working with other teachers in planning instructional sequences within subject–matter group meetings. The four units developed in this activity indicate the development of skills by the planners themselves. The first unit is the shortest and least sophisticated and the ensuing three indicate further depth of involvement and broader activities.

NUTRITION AND VITAMIN DEFICIENCY

A Unit for Ninth Grade General Science

I. Objectives
   A. To help students learn the relationship between good nutritional habits and health.

B. To develop a greater understanding of the relationship between good nutritional habits and health.

C. The development of personally meaningful habits of nutrition based on the first understanding.

II. Introductory Activity

Viewing of the film "And So They Live" (Indiana University Film Library, Bloomington, Indiana). Discussion of the standards and levels of living of these people and the poor nutritional habits experienced by these children as a result.

III. Developmental Activities

A. Reading from the textbook (**Health and Safety for You,** McGrawHill, 1965, pp. 241–302) of the importance of nutritional habits, the identification of kinds of health problems which will develop when various kinds of deficiencies take place over a long period of time in the eating habits of people.

B. An Experiment

An experiment performed by the teacher and the class in which a group of animals are fed diets varying in the deficiency of certain vitamins necessary to health. The purpose of this is to demonstrate dramatically the effects of certain vitamin deficiencies on animal fur and behavior over a period of time. Five groups of animals will be used as follows: The first group of animals will be fed a consistently normal diet throughout the entire period of experimentation. The second group of animals will be fed a diet deprived of vitamin A until the deficiencies appear in the behavior and condition of the animals. The animals in this group will then be fed a normal diet high in Vitamin A until their condition is restored to normalcy. Each of the other three groups will go through a similar experience except that different vitamins will be deprived and then restored in high quantity until the normal condition of the animal returns. The vitamins used for these groups will be B, D, and K. The experiment will be set up so that all students will be able to view and examine the fluctuations in the conditions of the animals during periods of deprivation of diet and of the return to diet with high amounts of the formerly deprived vitamin added to restore normal condition.

IV. Culminating Activities

A. The groups that worked with each of the five groups of animals for the experiment will report to the class at-large on the aspect of the experiment for which they were responsible. Conclusions will be identified as to the implications of prolonged deficiency of the kinds of vitamins and the kinds of problems which may be expected as the result of such deprivation. Upon the reports of these groups, the teacher will attempt to extend what effects deficiencies in humans might be from similar results and then present to the group what human problems would develop from such deprivation.

B. Teacher tests.

TOBACCO, ALCOHOL, AND NARCOTICS

Three Sub-Units for Seventh Grade Health

I. Over-All Objectives for the Three Sub-Units
  A. To instruct students as to the harmful effects of tobacco, alcohol, and narcotics on the body.
  B. To help students understand the use of and habituation to tobacco, alcohol, and narcotics.
  C. To help students develop some personally meaningful values and attitudes concerning contact with tobacco, alcohol, and narcotics.
  D. To help students develop understanding about the three areas of the sub-units as they are entering the period of adolescence which may well lead them to assume various roles in search of identity. Many adolescents assume habits for experimentation, in imitation of adults around them or because of a strong desire to do what their peers are doing. Smoking and drinking are solid examples of activities which the adult world wishes to discourage in teen-agers. Discussing the reasons why people do what they do with respect to smoking, drinking, and the use of narcotics gives substance to these three sub-units.

TOBACCO

I. Objectives for the Sub-Unit

  A. To understand that smoking has become a national habit because it fulfills various needs for different people.
  B. To show that despite its negative effects, smoking has positive values for many people. The impact of smoking has contributed to American economics through taxation, advertising, manufacturing and tobacco agriculture.
  C. To help students see the effect of the use of tobacco on health with reference to increasing medical evidence indicating that cancer of the lung, throat, and mouth as well as heart disease have dramatically greater incidence among smokers

as opposed to non–smokers.

II. Introductory Activity

View a film supplied by the Roswell Park Memorial Institute in Buffalo, New York, entitled, **Up in Smoke.** This film was designed to instruct students as to the harmful effects of pro- longed use of tobacco.

III. Developmental Activities

A. Classroom discussion. The class will be divided in half so that half will discuss reasons why people smoke as students perceive these reasons. The other half of the class will ques- tion the first half concerning some of the dilaterious side- effects of smoking, which, while they are not particularly dangerous are disturbing to some people. These include, stained fingers and teeth, dirty ash trays, tearing eyes and tobacco breath.

B. The teacher will blow cigarette smoke through a tissue and then lead discussion to identify the significance of the dis- coloring of the tissue in the human consumption of tobacco.

C. The class will read **Today's Health,** Laidlaw Brothers, 1963, pp. 150–160. Discussion of this information will precede the students writing out answers to questions contained at the end of that section of the text.

IV. Culminating Activities

A. Students will be organized into panel groups to research specific aspects of the information brought forth by the In- troductory and Developmental Activities. Library research and personal interviews with adults, in and out of school, regard- ing their smoking habits and attitudes toward smoking will be organized. Other groups will take a census regarding the smoking habits of adults as well as their adolescent peers. Reports will be given in class and articles will then be developed for student newspapers or interested community newspapers.

B. Teacher tests.

ALCOHOL

I. Objectives for the Unit

A. To understand the values of the use of alcohol. There are positive values for the use of alcohol, particularly medicinal ones, which are frequently overlooked, as well as the social values.

B. To understand the negative health effects of excess use of alcohol, including the psychotic syndrome developed with over–use of alcohol. These include Korsakoff's syndrome and the D. T.'s.

II. Introductory Activities

    A. Viewing of a film entitled **Control of Life,** from Alcoholics Anonymous followed by a discussion of the effects of alcohol by a representative of the organization.

III. Developmental Activities

    A. An experiment with either rats or cats. The first group of animals will be fed a small percentage of alcohol in a liquid which they normally take and their activities will be watched while the animals are under the influence of the alcohol. A second group of animals will be maintained on a normal diet and the differences between the two groups will be observed to show the effects of alcohol upon growth, learning habits, etc. With respect to the learning aspect of the experiment, the animals will be taught how to run a small maze in pursuit of a reward and the differences in the maze behavior will be dramatically observable. Following the habituation of the second group of animals to alcohol, they will be presented with milk or other liquid without alcohol in it and the reaction of the animals may be observed. Following this, the group of animals will be allowed to choose between liquid with alcohol and liquid without alcohol and their habituation will be recognizable.

    B. The class will be assigned to read the book **I'll Cry Tomorrow** by Lillian Roth. Following the reading, discussion will be held as to the accuracy and realism of the book in terms of what was viewed in the film and learned from the representative from Alcoholics Anonymous. Parallels through discussion can be made with the animal experiments to identify the degree to which animal behavior was parallel to human behavior as learned through reading and from the speaker.

    C. The class will be assigned library research on the alcohol industry of the United States and the importance of the amount of money collected by taxes on alcohol.

    D. Some members of the class will be selected to debate the pros and cons of lowering the legal age for drinking to 18 on a national scale or raising it on a national scale to age 21.

    E. Other members of the class will be assigned to research the era of prohibition and the problem of enforcement.

IV. Culminating Activities

    A. A debate will be held concerning the raising or lowering of the legal age for drinking to a national or regional level.

    B. Students will report on their library research on the alcohol industry and its total positive impact on the economy of the United States.

C. Teacher tests.

NARCOTICS

I. Objectives for this Unit
   A. To help students understand the positive and medicinal uses of narcotics.
   B. To help students understand the harmful effects of narcotics when they are not administered under medical supervision as in a situation of addiction.
   C. To help students understand the implications of narcotics traffic nationally and internationally and for the need of legalized control of the sale of narcotics.
   D. To help students understand the addiction of narcotics as a medical problem rather than as a crime and the societal need for such recognition.

II. Introductory Activity
   A. Listening to a record prepared by Synanon and the experiences of Joe Pass, an outstanding musician who became a narcotics addict, was rehabilitated and now works for the organization to educate the public regarding narcotics addiction. Distribution of written materials from Synanon for reading and discussion.

III. Developmental Activities
   A. Discussion of the nature of addiction to understand the differences between addiction and habituation and the identification of the problems of rehabilitation in each instance.
   B. Assign reading from **Today's Health,** Laidlaw Brothers, 1963, pages 160–184. Discussion of written materials to consider the mental health ramifications of drug addiction, and the social acceptance of the addict and the rehabilitated addict. This should lead to the consideration of the laws governing such people in the different states in the United States as opposed to those in European countries.
   C. Assign outside reading of **Monkey on My Back** by Barney Ross.
   D. Viewing of the film **Man with the Golden Arm.**
   E. Classroom experimentation. The teacher, through the school, will get permission of the local health officer to administer a narcotic to a rat and observe his reaction to electric shock. Another animal will be given similar shock treatment but without the introduction of the narcotic. A cat will be given catnip and put into planned situations for observed reaction,

following which another cat will be put through the same planned situations but without the introduction of catnip.

IV. Culminating Activities
   A. A student panel to be held on the social implications of narcotics and their legal and illegal use.
   B. A second student panel to consider how laws should be changed to govern the traffic of narcotics and the social implications of considering the narcotics addict as criminal or medical patient.

THE STUDY OF NUTRITION AND ITS RELATION TO CULTURE AND SOCIETY

A Unit for Ninth Grade Core with Reference for English Language-Arts, Social Studies and Health.

I. Objectives
   A. To demonstrate the relationship of nutrition to the various cultures of the world.
   B. To demonstrate the relationship of eating habits to religious philosophies.
   C. To demonstrate the relationship between eating habits and geography.
   D. To demonstrate the relationship between economic advertising and eating habits.
   E. To help students understand the interrelatedness of these areas in identifying the scope of this problem in terms of the importance not only of nutrition but of the emphasis which particular cultural patterns may have for particular cultures and societies in the development of their level or standard of health.

II. Introductory Activity
   A. A culinary experiment – have an assortment of foods representing both foods which come from different countries and foods which are commonly known to American students. The teachers will have the following prepared:
      1. Hot dogs cut in quarters and labeled as hot dogs.
      2. A plate of gefilte fish hors d'oeuvres so labeled.
      3. A plate of small cocktail Vienna sausages labeled Vienna sausages.
      4. A platter of Chinese foods containing egg foo yung and a whole, smoked baby sparrow on skewer labeled as such.
      5. A platter of Japanese food containing chocolate covered ants, fried grasshoppers, and diced octopus labeled as such.
      6. A platter of snails labeled as snails.

7. American diamond–back rattlesnake meat labeled as tuna fish.
8. A can of red Sock–eye salmon labeled as American diamond–back rattlesnake.

Each student will be requested to take a sampling of one food which he must eat. Enough of the hot dogs will be provided so that each of the students can take a piece if they desire. Each of the students will then be asked to make a statement as to why they chose the food they did after they selected and ate it. The teacher will then state exactly what each of the foods were, the country of origin and quickly establish a relationship, if there is an obvious one, between the food and the country of origin. For example, octopus is a product of the sea, and 80 per cent of the Japanese flesh diet comes from the sea because meat from land animals is extremely scarce. A specimen of processed, dried, edible seaweed will then be made available for sampling. This will indicate how the Japanese have made a palatable and delicious food from seaweed because of the relative scarcity of land grown vegetables. Even in developing delicacies, the Japanese have had to select such items from things which are relatively plentious in their environment.

The teacher will make a further statement concerning the choice or lack of coice of the diamond–back rattlesnake meat, the chocolate covered insects, etc. This statement will involve "natural" abhorance of people to try the unfamiliar or that which, although it may be perfectly acceptable on its merits, appears to be repulsive or objectionable in terms of the association which an individual develops in his own cultural environment. If a student ate from the can labeled diamond–back rattlesnake meat or from the can labeled tuna fish, the teacher will be able to dwell upon the impressions and reactions of the class. An understanding will be sought after here, especially if the individual may have enjoyed eating the rattlesnake meat when he thought it was tuna fish.

III. Developmental Activities
   A. Each of the students will be assigned a food, either germane to a country or representative of a cultural or ethnic group and assigned library research around the production of this food in relationship to the region of its origin and/or popularity. The following areas are to be assigned and researched:
       1. Lamb with Lebanon
       2. Pineapple with Hawaii
       3. Pasta with Italy
       4. Wine with France
       5. Cow with India
       6. Kashruth with Israel
       7. Oats with Scotland

8. Fish with Catholics
9. Rice with China
10. Black bread with Russia
11. Curry powder with India
12. Olives with Spain
13. Pasta with China
14. Enchiladas, tortillas, and tacos with Mexico
15. Potatoes with Ireland
16. Corn with America
17. Rabbit with Australia
18. Lobster with Maine
19. Chitterlings with the American Negro
20. Blubber with Alaskan Eskimo
21. Humans with New Guinea (cannibalism)
22. Cheese with Switzerland
23. Vodka with Russia
24. Bourbon with Kentucky
25. White bread with United States
26. Monkey with Africa
27. Soy bean flour with Korea
28. Tequila with Mexico
29. Hominy grits with southern United States
30. Rum with Puerto Rico

Students will develop the relationship between the various foods and the geography and/or culture of a country or a group of people with which the food is associated. The influence of certain foods or habits or customs of eating on disease and the economics of the country or people in terms of export or import should be stressed.

B. Students will report on their research of this activity and present individual, and in some cases, group reports, depending upon the number of students assigned to each one of the topics.

C. Areas of subject matter to be stressed by the teacher in his discussions or assignment of readings:

1. Geography - The study of geography here should seek to identify why customs of particular people have developed because of geographic factors, i.e., rice paddies in China, soy bean fields in Korea, goats in Switzerland, etc. Identification might be made as to how the customs or habits of people change when they migrate to different areas. Europeans who used various kinds of wheat and rye flour for baking in Europe have continued to enjoy products baked from these flours, but in the American setting, have developed a heavy utilization of maize or Indian corn which has now been domesticated into American

corn. Also, the use of bleached flour has developed primarily under American influence.

2. Government and Economics – The influence of the control of the government on the eating habits of people, i.e., the Food and Drug Administration in the United States, should be outlined. Also, examples should be drawn in instances where predominant cultural patterns of a people prevent the interference of government control even though the cultural patterns are bringing nutritional deficiencies to the people, i.e., the cow in India.

The American regulation of the production or curtailment of production under the soil bank can be considered from points of view of economic as well as governmental control. Stress should be made that while many foods can be produced cheaply in this country they are not accessible to all people because a specific item may be kept out of the purchasing range of a particular socio–economic group through the control of amounts of production, i.e., butter, oranges in the winter, beef, and pork. The implications of international trade barriers and the proven fact that America could produce enough food to feed the entire world, is another area to be stressed here.

3. Language–Arts – Selections from **Two Years before the Mast** by Richard Dana, may be read to indicate the accounts of nutritional problems which developed among sailors before food could be stored for long journeys as it is today. Selections from **Mutiny on the Bounty** by Nordloff and Hall may be read to consider the problems of cannibalism in remote societies. The writing of themes, self–creative in approach concerning the meaning of food to them or their food habits, as for example, the traditional American Thanksgiving turkey dinner or the Friday night Sabbath for the Jews.

IV. Culminating Activities

A. Each student will survey his parents and family on the kinds of foods they purchase and the types of foods which, perhaps, they do not purchase and interpret these purchases in terms of cultural biases and economic limitations. These reports should be typewritten and submitted anonymously to be read at–large to the class to indicate what unknown individuals in the class may face in the way of limitations of their eating habits for one reason or another.

B. Panel discussion by students in an attempt to identify what attitudes and learnings have been gained through the unit.

C. Teacher tests.

DEMOCRACY - HOW IT AFFECTS PEOPLE

A Unit for World History

I. Objectives

A. To provide a background of knowledge concerning democracy as political and social organization.

B. To help youngsters understand that democracy, like all other political and social institutions, has weaknesses as well as strengths.

C. To help youngsters understand the implications of democracy for the individual in society as well as the needs of society at-large.

D. To help youngsters appreciate the problems of democracy not only in specific historic instances, but to bring this information to bear upon the problems of democracy in the world today.

E. To provide the student with actual experience in participating in a democracy through his experiences in the school.

F. Understandings to be sought after in this unit. Students are expected to go forth from school into adult life and be able to function as intelligent participants in a democratic society. Schools, unfortunately, may teach about democracy but do either relatively little to help the student learn about the roles which he should fulfill as an intelligent participant in a democratic society, or how to perform these roles. The typical American secondary school, unfortunately, is a better practical experience of an authoritarian, totalitarian society than it is as a growing experience for students who are hopefully to become the aforementioned intelligent participants in a democratic society. This unit seeks to develop the realization that learning about something is not necessarily learning that topic itself or how to take the information and apply it in an operational setting. Learning about democracy, in specific instances, in World History, should serve to: (1) appreciate the life and times of the historical past and the progress which people made during these times and (2) bring these understandings to bear for the student to better understand and be able to operate, even as a student, as a participant in a democratic climate and to appreciate the problems of democracy in the world today.

II. Introductory Activities

A. Initial reading assignment to cover the organization and structure of Athenian society. As the first introductory activity, students would be assigned this for reading outside of class.

B. The following day, a teacher-led discussion would be developed reviewing the material and identifying the important emphases which were necessarily instituted in Athenian society. Questions are to be assigned to students outside of class which will be designed to help them develop statements identifying the strengths and weaknesses in terms of fair, human society as the day's discussion had revealed it to exist in Athenian society.

III. Developmental Activities

A. Students in the class are to be divided into several groups representing the societal makeup of Athenian society. Seventy per cent of the class will be designated as slaves and five per cent of the class as the scholars, Plato, Socrates, etc. Twenty per cent of the class are to be designated as the affluent citizenry of Athens and five per cent of the class designated as the governmental leadership and the military leadership. After this designation, groups other than the slaves, are to be assigned into committees with references of library materials to be considered for study and reporting in class. The 70 per cent of the class, designated as slaves, will do the work needed to develop the reports by the other groups. As slaves, they have no choice but to go through the experience and follow the dictates of the groups.

B. The groups do their research and have the physical work of organizing it done by the slave culture.

C. Further reading of text and other reading materials on the historical growth, flourishing, and decline of Athenian society are pursued independently of the group activities.

D. The teacher will present, for discussion, the writings and impact of the writings of the scholars of the class at-large.

E. Teacher to prepare a lecture on democracy as a philosophy of social and political organization as opposed to actual forms of political and social organization. Students, here, need to understand that Athens was not a democracy, but an attempt at a democratic approach to life, and that the United States is not a democracy, but a constitutional republic. There is a spirit of democracy and a democratic approach to the way of life in both settings. However, both achieved different levels of attainments because of the evolution of the human race in the instance of each culture's existence.

F. The class will be divided into six groups. Each group is to consider a country or countries in the contemporary world as they reflect an approach to democratic government. The first group will consider the United States as a democratic form of government and identify how it has either fallen prey to or gone beyond limitations of the spirit of democracy identified in Athenian culture. The second group shall apply this to West Germany, the third group shall apply this to Israel, a fourth group shall apply this to Japan, a fifth group to the Congo Republic, and the sixth group to the Union of South Africa.

G. Students will write a composition on one of the following topic areas:

1. The United States, Israel, and West Germany have made definite strides in attaining specific advantages for their citizens through democratic forms of government. Selecting one of these countries, students will identify and discuss what are some of the most important objectives of democratic government which the country has failed to achieve.

2. Japan has achieved dramatic success in a score of years under a democratic form of government following generations of deity worship. Students will identify and discuss some of the major social reforms developed during the past 20 years.

3. The Congo is considered by many to be a Republic which has attempted to move too rapidly toward a democratic form of government because her people are not sufficiently westernized so as to live in a westernized society. The Union of South Africa is still based upon what many consider to be a slave base. If this is true then it appears to be done with a moral awareness which differs from Athenian society which did not have such an awareness. Students are to select one of these countries and identify and discuss what kinds of social progress for individual rights should be the major concern of that country in providing basic human rights for her citizens.

4. Students will identify what has democracy, as an approach to political and social organization, gained and grown from the experiences and achievements of Athenian Society? Students will support their answers with references to contemporary nations embracing democratic forms of government.

5. Students will take a position on whether or not the United Nations is a truly democratic approach to world government? If so, students must identify if the philosophical approach of the United Nations shows a bias against governments of the world which are other than democratic in their orientation and structure?

IV. Culminating Activities

A. The class will report and discuss its experiences as "members of Athenian Society."

B. Groups organized under III.F, will report to the class.

C. Teacher tests.

F. Consulting Teacher Services

This aspect of "THE COORDINATED APPROACH" was an extension of function as well as the broadening of one. In the extension, it brought the curriculum supervisor more frequently into the classroom as a consultant. In such situations the teacher might request help, might plan a unit of work with the supervisor, with the supervisor teaching parts of the unit so that the teacher might observe, and the supervisor being invited to teach a lesson on special topics in which he had specific skill. Under the approaches to the implementation of "THE COORDINATED APPROACH," the supervisor continued his regular program of classroom observations. The identification of the skills of the school psychologist led to the agreement that a preventive approach to curriculum planning could best benefit from the involvement of the psychologist with his specialization in the psychology of human learning. At the same time, the feelings of confidence in the psychologist gained through classroom visitation with resultant conferences led the broadening of the concept of teacher consultant services to include the psychologist. To facilitate the psychologist's further acceptance by the faculty in classroom visitation, situations were identified in which the psychologist might be able to contribute as a teacher, as a consultant with a degree of expertness beyond what the teacher might possess.

This was inadvertently facilitated by an English teacher's asking if anyone in the school could serve as an expert on Sigmund Freud in conjunction with her group's study of the evolution of psychology in the 20th century European setting. The psychologist prepared a two-period lecture and was enthusiastically received by the students and teacher. The success of this experience and the comments made by the teacher involved, prompted another teacher of English to ask the psychologist to come in and interpret the influence of modern psychology, particularly Freud, upon the writings of Ernest Hemingway. A third experience involved the psychologist going into two additional English classes, once to discuss the psychological implications of the guilt of Lady MacBeth in the Shakespearean play and on another occasion, the concept of guilt as developed in "The Secret Sharer" by Joseph Conrad.

In other instances, the psychologist was called upon to perform this teacher-consultant service in 7th and 10th grade health classes with regard to mental health and its importance, and problems of mental health in the American society today.

While part of the usual function of the curriculum supervisor is to go into classrooms and give demonstration lectures, pointing out various techniques of teaching, various approaches which teachers of the different subjects might use, it is not nearly as often that the typical school psychologist is called into a classroom to teach. It is true that his skills are primarily in the field of mental health, but the field of mental health bridges a tremendous area in the society in which we live. Thus, the psychologist need not be used only typically in health classes or in courses in adolescent psychology or in related subject matter, but he may be used in areas quite distantly removed from the usual sphere of psychology. It should be apparent that the psychologist can, very comfortably, be used in the study of literature, in American History, or for that matter, the history of various periods of society. He can be used in general science courses in the discussion of scientific methodology and he should be used as an available resource person. There is no reason why the psychologist could not be used in French or Spanish or German or other foreign language classes to help the students recognize how speech typically develops.

It should be obvious that the whole thesis of this text is one which says schools have resources. These resources should be used wherever possible. In this particular case, the curriculum supervisor also happens to be a musician with symphonic, jazz, folk, and popular musical experience. At first glance, it may seem to the reader that this particular talent is not usable in the school system except, perhaps, in music education. Unfortunately, such thinking has led to considerable stereotypy in education. The creative aspect in education is the careful appraisal of every talent that is available, talent that the pupil has, talent that the teacher has, and in using such talent. Therefore, the curriculum supervisor was used not as a curriculum supervisor, but as a musician in a number of programs around folk music and the relationship of folk music to the times in which the students live. The precedent set here was not the teaching of music, but the utilization of the curriculum supervisor's skills as a teacher and his background in music to identify key aspects of impact in various subject matter areas. In the area of American History, a unit of study was presented on "Jazz as America's Only Native-Developed, Cultural Entity." This dealt with the real significance of the "melting-pot process" wherein values, folkways, and the cultural heritages of European and Asian cultures, as brought to this country by immigrants, contributed to the evolution of this American musical art form. Beyond this, the area of American Jazz has had great implications for social progress through the integration of races, ethnic groups, and ideas. Thus again, the focus was not upon the curriculum supervisor's skills as a musician, but as a teacher borrowing from an area of erudite knowledge as it might be focused upon areas of the established curriculum which were difficult to crystallize in the minds of students. Other areas in which the supervisor functioned were General Science, where various laws of Physics could be identified as they applied to the sending and utilization of sound waves in the creation of music as captured by the human ear; junior high school social studies in which the music and musical ideas of various world cultures were used to mirror some of the social practices within these cultures at-large themselves; health classes in which the development of musical fads by various American generations are identified as they provided an emotional release and expression for adolescent peer groups in various generations. This latter area was done cooperatively with the psychologist.

Thus, the curriculum supervisor expanded his consultant function into new areas and at the same time worked with the psychologist to identify areas in which his particular skills, not only as an expert in human learning, but in human behavior, generally, could be brought into focus in consultant and teaching experiences which would directly involve students as well as teachers in the classroom.

The purpose of the consulting teacher service, to repeat, is to emphasize the values gained in using all of the staff available in the school. There is no doubt but that the custodian has something to offer to the teaching situation. Should the reader search himself and find "no" skills which might be used outside of his knowledge of content area, then the reader is not creating. He is hiding behind the stereotyped, rigid view that content area is subject matter and nothing else. A well educated person is an individual who is able to use his knowledge from the various fields he has studied in many different ways. He need not persist in using the same old approach day in and day out.

G. Special Class Planning

The special class presently under discussion is not a class for children with retarded intellectual development, but rather a class for youngsters who, in the 7th and 8th grade, were found to be grossly underachieving with near normal or dull-normal intelligence. These were children who presented very special learning problems in the sense, particularly, that they were fed up with failure experience. Much of their elementary school experience led them to believe that they were not competent and perhaps they were not, in the strictly academic program. These children attended a class-room situation which was more contained than departmentalized. Two teachers were involved in the 7th and 8th grade slow learner program. The programs were self-contained to the point that in 7th grade the students studied English, Language-Arts, Social Studies, Mathematics, and Health with the self-contained classroom situation. They did leave the room for Art, Music, Homemaking, Industrial Arts, and Science. At the same time, another teacher was involved with the 8th grade group and these two people worked in close proximity together planning their program with the school psychologist and the curriculum supervisor. Each teacher followed the group for two consecutive years.

It must be remembered that these youngsters had been quite unsuccessful in the typical school situation. Much of what they were exposed to had little meaning to them in terms of their everyday lives. When they entered the 7th grade, many of them felt that they could never succeed in school and had completely given up. Others had strengths in some areas and very serious weaknesses in others, especially reading. The classes were deliberately relatively small so that the youngsters would have as much individual attention as possible.

The authors believe that the way to a pupil's learning-heart is through meaning. If what he is exposed to has meaning for him in his everyday existence, he is far more likely to cope with the responsibilities of learning, and far more likely to see some success. With this in mind, the teachers of these special classes met frequently with the authors to plan approaches and share techniques which might be of value to the students involved. In these frequent discussions, a number of things became evident very quickly.

First of all, soon after these youngsters came into the 7th grade setting, they became very much aware of the fact that their classes were not departmentalized but self-contained. They asked why they were different and it was obvious that a realistic and honest answer had to be given to them. The psychologist worked closely with both teachers in helping them talk frankly with the pupils about their "difference" from the other 7th and 8th grade pupils. These students called themselves "retards" and had very definite attitudes about themselves which were not all complimentary and not necessarily realistic, at least in some respects. They were not retarded children and considerable effort was expended in helping them accept the fact that they were not retarded intellectually, but slower and behind academically. The psychologist was asked to come into the classes directly and carry on group discussions with the students concerning how they were different and what this difference meant to them and what it might mean in the future. These youngsters had, in the past, been told by teachers and by their own parents that if they worked harder they would do better, that really all they had to do was study and behave, etc. It was pointed out to them that this kind of activity on their part would go a long way towards helping them improve their skills, but it was not the answer. They had to face and accept the fact that they were slower intellectually. Accepting this would make it easier for them to face the fact that they would have to put forth added effort to achieve.

There were a number of purposes involved in creating these particular special classes. These youngsters were seen as immature emotionally as well as intellectually. Many of them were quite unable to assume an independent role in terms of their own academic responsibilities. Many of them needed considerable constructive leadership to help them plan for their work, to show them how they might use reference material, how they might help each other cooperatively, etc. This involved consultations with the curriculum supervisor as well as the school psychologist.

For a number of the boys in these classes, certain practical skills held considerable interest for them. They were interested in wiring light plugs, for example, and needed some knowledge of electricity. To discuss electricity with these students in a completely abstract sense, was a waste of time. To discuss it in the context of its meaning for household wiring and simple repair work, made the abstract far more concrete and meaningful. This kind of approach was used in a number of areas. It was used successfully in social studies with map reading; it was used in building arithmetic skills, especially the handling of fractions, etc.

Goals for this class were considered carefully by pupil personnel, guidance people as well as the teachers involved, the curriculum supervisor and school psychologist. Planning for the future of these youngsters in terms of the remaining years of their high school program was cooperatively held. This kind of relationship helped the two teachers involved feel that they were being given considerable support in the handling of these classes.

Some of these children had difficulties with motor coordination manifested by problems in writing and copying. Some of them also had difficulties in visual reproduction of form. In the diagnostic experience which the psychologist had, the use of colored crayons and bright colored pencils was often found to be helpful to many such children in delineating form. The teachers were told about the use of colored crayons and pencils and were also told that careful use of color has been found helpful in teaching children long division (using a different color for each arithmetic process) or in emphasizing certain spelling rules and in any situation in which the youngster's focus and attention is demanded. Such techniques were found to be helpful with some of these youngsters to some degree. This kind of assistance to the teachers represented an attempt to use skills of the psychologist which might otherwise not be utilized and certainly would not be utilized without close working relationship between the teachers and the psychologist.

Attempts were made to create an interesting program for these pupils, but one that would be concrete rather than abstract. Thus, as was seen in the case of the light plug and electricity, every effort was made to use audio-visual techniques. Building with wood, hammer and nails, enlarged maps constructed by the students using battery-operated small cars, were among suggestions made.

In teaching social studies, it was suggested that a more concrete, meaningful understanding of the problem of taxation, working together, developing laws for the purposes of regulating society, etc. could best be understood if the students were placed in a situation which would involve their depending upon these relatively abstract concepts. It was suggested that the students' seats be arranged so that each seat represented a particular state of the Union. The floors of the room would be outlined in colored paper and each student would have the privilege of imposing taxation, penalties, and the like whenever another student wished to cross his property to get from one place to another. This definitely made concrete an experience which otherwise was likely to have very little meaning in the present life experience of the youngster.

In the follow-up to the understanding of the important concepts made operational in the American government under the Constitution as opposed to the Articles of Confederation, the teacher asked the students if they wanted to participate in an experiment in undemocratic living. The students were interested and willing to experiment. The teacher, who had been very fair in terms of trying to organize the interests of students in this program, became completely autocratic with regard to the structure of the classroom, its atmosphere, learning activities selected, instructional materials, and all privileges of students. Students were not allowed to go to the lavatory for a day and forced to act completely upon the whim and discretion of the teacher. The group rebelled, but since they had agreed to participate in the experiment, were sufficiently proud as to follow it through despite the very trying experience which it proved for many of them as individuals. What happens in non-totalitarian society when an absolutist government takes over the society was paralleled in a concept quite well understood and assimilated by the group.

As indicated earlier, the authors were often called into classes to serve as consulting teachers. An opportunity to serve one of the special classes arose early in the semester when the teacher took advantage of the civil rights difficulties in integrating certain of the Southern public schools. She had asked the youngsters in her class what their feelings would be if, upon coming to school, they were met by state troopers and not permitted to enter the school for one reason or another. Her thought was to begin the study of civil rights and help these students understand what some of the problems were inherent in the civil rights activities as well as to come to an understanding of the basic issue of prejudice. She felt lacking in her own understanding of prejudice and asked the psychologist to come into her class for one or two sessions to discuss with the group how prejudice arises. It must be remembered that this is a group best able to cope with the abstract if the abstract is made concrete. The psychologist went into the classroom for two periods and discussed with them the origin of prejudice by using the analogy of **Blue Mashed Potatoes.** In psychological research many years ago, it was shown that people chose foods to eat not only by their knowledge of those foods and the tastes of those foods, but also on the basis of expected color and appearance. The students in the classroom admitted to liking mashed potatoes and admitted also to expecting that mashed potatoes would have its characteristic white color. They were asked to consider what their behavior and attitudes would be when presented with a dish of mashed potatoes colored with a tasteless vegetable coloring, blue. The students unanimously refused to consider eating such mashed potatoes. They made facial grimaces, they giggled, they were somewhat excited at the prospect and at the same time, repelled. They were, however, able to talk quite freely about the fact that they would not eat these mashed potatoes and were perfectly certain that they would not like them. It's obvious how the analogy with the civil rights problem could be drawn. It's also obvious that in discussing this abstract problem in concrete terms, these students could become very animated and comprehend a problem which they might not otherwise even express interest in because it would, at first glance, appear to be far removed from their own realm of thinking.

Functioning in a coordinated way, this kind of class is given help it would not otherwise get. The psychologist's contributions do not end with placement of the pupils. They begin here by using her knowledge of the interests, assets, and liabilities of each pupil in developing a program of study for these youngsters that is realistic in meeting their needs. Curricular activity is planned by the teacher with the contributions of the curriculum supervisor and the school psychologist. When the teacher feels she has a problem she cannot deal with comfortably, she has the security of knowing help is available.

CHAPTER III

REQUIREMENTS FOR
"THE COORDINATED APPROACH"
A PHILOSOPHY

A. Curriculum Supervisor and School Psychologist Leadership Roles

The development of the "THE COORDINATED APPROACH" was not accidental. The germ of the idea grew from the discussions which the curriculum supervisor and the school psychologist held with each other in an attempt to identify their own specific roles and functions within the school Setting. As they discussed what these roles were, they became aware of overlapping of function as well as omissions of function. This was discussed in Chapter I.

Out of the frequent and rather lengthy discussions which took place, the authors became aware of a number of different objectives which they felt it was necessary for the school system to achieve in order to provide the students with a wide variety of educational experiences in a setting conducive to learning. They spelled these objectives out and these became the objectives of "THE COORDINATED APPROACH." They were as follows:

1. to develop a school-wide awareness of the needs for a broadly articulated all-school program with the greatest possible interaction of all the skills and abilities of the entire faculty and school staff.

2. to develop a perceptive awareness by the entire faculty and school staff of the symptoms of behavioral disturbance and of disturbances in learning as they occur in the K through 12 program.

3. to develop teacher sensitivity and awareness of these problems so that continuous curriculum planning activity may seek to establish a preventive approach as these problems continue to be identified and referred for consideration and alleviation.

4. to identify the roles which teachers and specialists may play in cooperatively approaching the solution to these problems.

5. to establish this all-school program toward the increasing prevention of school-created disturbances in learning and behavior.

6. to develop a school-wide program from experiences in the curricula of the school through comprehensive curriculum planning activities which will seek to be preventive in terms of avoiding or alleviating situations in which behavioral disturbances and disturbances in learning have been identified as occurring.

7. to organize instructional services and pupil personnel services generally, and the activities of the curriculum supervisor and the school psychologist specifically for study of the curriculum in action, individual teacher counselling, group therapy and in-service workshops for planning curricular programs to operationalize a preventive approach to curriculum planning and the organization of instruction.

The achievement of these objectives appear to the authors to be worthy of tremendous effort in organizing an all-school program which can make such achievement possible. To do this meant that the authors had to assume leadership roles, not only in their individual working relationships with the faculty and staff of the school, but also in working together as a unit to impress upon the remaining school faculty that coordination not only was possible but was advisable. Thus, the coordinated effort began within the working relationship of the curriculum supervisor and the school psychologist and served as an example for the remainder of the faculty.

It was necessary for each of the authors to assume a role of leadership with each other as well as with the remainder of the faculty. The curriculum supervisor had to identify aspects of the curriculum and the all-school program in which the psychologist needed to become involved with regard to analyzing problems in learning as well as areas of student frustration. His specialization in curriculum planning, instructional techniques and methodology had to be brought to cooperative consideration with the psychologist. At the same time his knowledge of individual teachers and their strengths and weaknesses as teachers, the strengths and weaknesses of departmental programs and the degree to which they were able to consider the improvement of such programs and the alleviation of problems were important areas with which the psychologist had to become meaningfully involved.

The curriculum supervisor must then assume a leadership role in educating the school psychologist in the area of curriculum planning, instructional methodology and techniques, subject-matter organization, and in other areas of background and information with which the psychologist will need to become involved.

The curriculum supervisor, by the nature of his position, has the closest and most confidential relationship with teachers of any person on the professional staff. From this position he should be able to develop a leadership role in helping teachers gain an understanding of what the psychologist may be able to contribute and of gaining acceptance of this specialist by teachers in a contributing role and not as a "head-shrinker." The curriculum supervisor can assume a leadership role in educating the psychologist in the area of curriculum planning skill, instructional methodology and techniques, subject-matter organization and other areas of background information with which the psychologist will need to become involved for specific aspects of "THE COORDINATED APPROACH." So that the psychologist can work more effectively with curriculum planning at the teacher level, the interpretation of prescribed course regulations by the State and other jurisdictional areas must be identified. The identification of what constitutes a curriculum guide and a course outline for a particular subject-matter experience must be made in terms of the necessities demanded by the grade level and/or subject-matter area being taught by the Teacher. Basic skills and the organization of content areas into curriculum guides and grade level planning are other areas which the curriculum supervisor can identify for the psychologist. The importance and scope of curriculum planning activities and the actual activities themselves which may be organized and implemented on a teacher-to-teacher, grade level, subject-matter area, building-wide, level-wide, and system-wide basis are other areas to be instructed by the curriculum supervisor. Proven techniques and established procedures in such activities as well as the identification of proper roles and involvement of students and lay population in such activities are further areas of expertness which the curriculum supervisor can share in working with the psychologist. Unit planning, resource unit planning, and the organization of instructional materials in terms of learning sequences can also be interpreted by the curriculum supervisor. Thus, the techniques, materials, and organization of the instructional program and activities are an area of expertness which the curriculum supervisor must bring into the awarenesses and background of the school psychologist for them to successfully work together in such a cooperative adventure.

The psychologist, in his participation in this kind of coordinated effort, must identify aspects of pupil development at all levels, primary through secondary, so that such development will be related to curriculum planning and to instructional techniques. This means that the psychologist must help the curriculum supervisor be cognizant of the meaning of deviation in development as such deviation affects and is affected by the school curriculum at all levels. He must help the curriculum supervisor train the teachers with regard to the necessity for individualized instructional techniques around certain kinds of special problems as, for example, might be found with a brain damaged child. But perhaps his greatest role involves helping the curriculum supervisor see the relationship within the classroom of the teacher–pupil interaction and success in teaching those pupils. In addition, the psychologist is in a position to help the curriculum supervisor work on a group basis with his teachers, helping him to develop an awareness of the emotional involvements of teachers in their working relationships with authority figures, with parents, with their colleagues as well as with their pupils.

It can be seen that the curriculum specialist and the psychologist must explain and reexplain to each other, not only what their functions are but perhaps what their training is and the way in which they view children and the learning process. Because of the difference in their training and backgrounds, the view is often different. This difference should not be ignored, but rather advantage should be taken of it as a stimulus for further growth.

The leadership aspect of this program lies in the fact that those who undertake it cannot remain hidden behind an isolated view of what the role each person has happens to be. It is much easier to keep from sticking your neck out than it is to institute a new thought or a new idea even if there really is not anything new involved. Threat is to be dealt with when any new program gets under way. To the teacher who remains standing in front of her classroom dealing with twenty or thirty very different kinds of youngsters, a new program means that she has something to learn, and by inference it means something she does not already know. This very often produces defensiveness for the teacher is threatened and is not perceived as knowing what she is supposed to do or how she is supposed to deal. The curriculum supervisor and school psychologist must convey to the receiving teachers as well as to the pupils and to the administrative faculty, that if there is threat perceived, it is perceived because there is too much complacency or inadequacy. Resistance to change may arise out of rigidity and if it does it is defensive. The leadership roles of the curriculum supervisor and the school psychologist will not necessarily reflect administrative authority. They must, however, reflect the authority that comes with knowledge and experience.

In many respects the job of the curriculum supervisor and the school psychologist remains easier if it does not arouse anyone. As long as the curriculum supervisor remains hidden beneath a tremendous number of textbooks at various grade levels, books which he is perusing with the idea of adopting them for the classes, he keeps out of trouble. As long as the school psychologist deals with I.Q.'s and other test data, he keeps out of trouble. Neither one accomplishes all he can in this kind of isolated endeavor.

B. Administration: Understandings for Cooperation

It has often been said that a school is as good as its teachers. Undoubtedly, this is an oversimplification, for while the classroom teacher may be the backbone of the school, the function, tone, and morale of the school is set by the administration. We are all quite well aware that the ways in which administrators delegate responsibility, the ways in which a change is considered and evolved, the ways in which teachers are observed and taught, parents are respected and children are treated, are the ways in which the administration reflects not just its philosophy of education but its respect for education.

No program, new or old, practical or experimental, can effectively operate without the administration's whole understanding and strong support. Obviously, this is essential to the creation of a program such as suggested by "THE COORDINATED APPROACH." Let us consider, for example, an administrator's conception of the services of the school psychologist. Typically, it is a deviant child who comes to the attention of the teacher or the administrator––a child perhaps not achieving as expected, or perhaps a discipline problem––a child who needs "something," but who for one reason or another stands out in class as special or different. The typical request for help involves a "test." The "test," unfortunately, is regarded by too many administrators as holding all the answers (and, of course, it does look good in the child's folder or the teacher's file!). If this is the administrator's perception of the typical school psychologist, then the kind of programs suggested in this writing cannot be instituted without re–educating the administrator. It should also be clearly stated that this kind of expectation leads the administrator to view the school psychologist as a mystic who is not terribly helpful, but who, as a special service of the school, adds some status and prestige to the roster of its special services.

In order to institute a program such as suggested here, the administration has to understand what strengths there are in taking an all–school, all–services preventive approach. The administration must understand that there are many difficulties to be encountered, responsibilities to be faced, and pressures to be dealt with. Holding parents responsible for the maladjustments of their children may be realistic, for parents undoubtedly contribute to the problems their children have. However, the assumption must also be made that the school is a force upon all children with whom it deals. If it is not a force, then it can have no impact upon the child--and it follows, it can teach him nothing.

Thus, the administrative staff must consider and accept the notion that prevention involves not just the early recognition of pupil problems (and necessary testing) but that changes recommended are likely to involve many different school personnel regardless of what other changes and recommendations there are involving extra school people. Re-evaluation of attitudes and expectations may involve not just parents and child but teachers and child. The straw that breaks the camel's back may be the straw that is put on in school.

Prevention necessitates the participation of classroom teachers and special teachers in conferences around a particular pupil, in general in-service programs stressing child development in the educational setting, in providing for group discussion of attitudes and values, as well as teaching techniques. It involves the creation of an atmosphere stressing a healthy exchange of information through which the participants share their tricks of the trade, their successful techniques, their, "this is what worked for me," as well as their honest concerns and struggles with innovations and stubborn problems. It involves placing the new teacher not in isolation to struggle alone, but in a context where help is not only available but freely offered. This means that administration must provide leadership and direction. If administration is weak, the school may run itself but it is not likely to go anywhere.

For the purposes of the present program, the administration must be able and willing to delegate responsibility and assign reasonable authority to the cooperating leaders who develop the program. They must provide support and enthusiasm. They must be aware of the needs of their faculty and respect these needs. They must accept teachers as professionals, and treat them so.

Relative to this point, we are all aware that teachers are not enthusiastic about attending after-school meetings. It is unfortunately true that many school faculty meetings are a waste of time and energy for all concerned except the person who conducts the meeting. For him there is some compensation, usually in the form of an opportunity to exercise authority. But the kinds of involvement of teachers suggested here depends upon energetic motivation and genuine interest. The meeting has to be rewarding!

With this in mind and on the basis of the authors' experience, two points come clearly into focus. The first is that participation by the teachers must be voluntary. If a teacher does not want to come to an in-service workshop or group discussion, forcing him to do so is a guarantee of resistance, passive or otherwise. It makes no difference how often we know that the teacher who "needs it the most is the one most unlikely to come." This teacher's attitude is bound to be contagious. On the other hand, though far fewer teachers may participate in the voluntary program, the fact that they are motivated serves to make the leader's function more successful, and if the leader does a better job, the meeting has more meaning for everyone. This, too, is contagious and this contagion will also be spread.

The second point is too often overlooked. It may seem ridiculous to consider the comfort aspects of those people involved in participating in the program. However, in-service work generally takes place after school hours. Teachers are tired, group leaders are tired, everyone is tired. It does not take much to set up a coffee urn and to provide doughnuts or cookies to offer some means by which people participating might kick off their shoes and relax a little.

If the administration understands and accepts this emphasis on prevention, it has the capacity and the authority to run quite a "sale." How successful the sale is certainly depends upon the commodity to be sold, but interest in the commodity must be created through the enthusiastic support of the school's administrators. Teachers are not blind followers in spite of some justifiable criticism. They do have a "show-me" attitude and it rests upon the school's leaders to do just that. Areas of communication and coordination must be opened. In essence, then, the broad implications of "THE COORDINATED APPROACH" must be wholeheartedly acceptable to the school administration which must assume the obligation of administering the program. While the leaders would still come into focus as authority figures by the nature of their special skills and their leadership functions in the program, all "legal" organization and authority would come to be the responsibility of the administration. This makes possible closer identification between the group leader and the participants, an identification based upon the leaders' abilities to give of their knowledge and special skills and to create situations in which the efficiency of relationships between the leaders and the teachers is improved. This identification is a real catalyst, a boon to improved communication for all concerned.

Failure to achieve the broad understanding and acceptance of the kind of program here suggested does not mean that the program cannot be at all implemented. It does mean that the initial task is two-fold--first, that the administration must become aware of the duplication of services within the school as well as gaps existing within and between tangential services. An immediate awareness of economic waste and functioning inefficiency should result. Schools have many specialists available--reading consultants, speech teachers, social workers, nurse–teachers, attendance officers, and guidance counselors, to name but a few. These people cannot work in a vacuum and be effective. All of these and other special services must coordinate their efforts with each other and the classroom teacher to function as a **whole** school dealing with a **whole** child. The administration must become more fully aware of the way in which these special services can work together to offer the school the best of their combined abilities. Secondly, a beginning attempt to demonstrate selected aspects of this program can be made by working in a single school rather than across the entire system. The school chosen should obviously be under the guidance of a principal who sees the merit of the coordinated effort. If merit is perceived by the teachers, then the program will sell itself. Once a successful, spirited program is established, other schools in the system become curious, interested, threatened, and challenged. Growth and change evolve this way!

C. Guidance and Pupil Personnel: Understandings for Co-operation

Within this setting, the school psychologist worked as a member of the pupil personnel staff. This situation might not hold in other school settings. It is not at all uncommon for the school psychologist to be directly responsible to the supervising principal or school superintendent, especially in relatively small school systems. In instances where the psychologist is not operating within the scope of pupil personnel services, basic understanding should be striven for through first, administration and secondly, through guidance and pupil personnel services themselves.

The primary objective of "THE COORDINATED APPROACH" is to bring pupil personnel and instructional services into close co-operation. In order to facilitate this and to achieve the broadening of the functions of the psychological services, particularly toward a preventive approach, the psychological services must of necessity be considered to be part of and operationally to function as part of the pupil personnel services. While it may really make little difference under whose aegis the school psychologist fuctions, the functioning of the school psychologist in cooperation with the curriculum supervisor and other staff members, remains a most fruitful avenue of approach for the prevention of school–initiated, school–related problems.

The development of understanding at this level may evolve in one of two ways, the first being most desirable. The most positive approach toward developing the kind of understanding and cooperation necessary to facilitate the implementation of "THE CO-ORDINATED APPROACH" is to develop necessary understandings, initially, with the pupil personnel staff and especially the director of such services. It is felt that most competent pupil personnel staff members, especially guidance counselors, should be quite readily able to perceive the need for cooperation between the instructional services and the counselling services, including those services represented by the curriculum supervisor and the school psychologist. Literature in both guidance and counselling and curriculum development more and more recommends such cooperation and identifies the rationale for it. The alternative approach towards developing the necessary understandings for implementation of "THE COORDINATED APPROACH" may have to come through administration. This is not considered to be the best way of achieving this understanding, since it suggests that the pupil personnel people may not hold to the kind of philosophy which is presented here and which would be necessary for coordination of special services at all levels. However, it is known that in certain schools pupil personnel services have not reached the sophistication necessary to implement the program suggested here. In such cases, unfortunately, the directive would have to come through administration.

Pupil personnel services basically seek to help the student adjust to the school's program, its curriculum, and demands of the all-school program. The area of curriculum planning and supervision seeks to organize the program, curricula, and the demands of the school more adequately to meet the needs of the students served by the school. The psychologist, of course, deals with the student who has not been able to make the necessary adjustment. It would seem obvious that coordination of the all-school program and cooperation by the school's specialized services would have to be a natural outgrowth of the objectives of the pupil personnel staff, curriculum supervisor, and school psychologist. However, all too often each of these individual specialists works separately and the coordination which is necessary for the fullest growth of the student does not take place.

As with the administrative level, there is an aspect of orientation and in-service education involving pupil personnel staff which must be planned by the curricular supervisor and the psychologist. One of the assumptions made initially in this book is that often staff members do not know what other staff members do. Thus, it is absolutely essential that the curriculum supervisor, the psychologist and the pupil personnel staff or director of guidance expend considerable energy explaining to each other the functions and services which each of these individuals offer to the school. Development of this interchange will also necessitate the consideration of a philosophical approach to the operation of the pupil personnel services which will make a definite commitment to cooperation with instructional services and planning aspects of "THE COORDINATED APPROACH." In involving the pupil personnel services in examining and developing this kind of coordinated organization, commitment of counselors and other pupil personnel specialists to the support of this program may readily be gained. This, of course, is considered by the authors to be a prerequisite for establishing a workable and successful program.

Guidance services, whether at the secondary level or at the all-school level, encompass more than the development of a schedule for individual pupils, which may or may not change as pupil needs change. They involve pupil personnel counselling, teacher instruction, the involvement of school nurse-teachers in health aspects of the program, attendance workers, social workers, etc., all of whom focus on the needs of the individual pupil. These persons all represent aspects of a well organized pupil personnel department. The cooperation necessary here from the director of pupil personnel services involves his freeing the psychologist and other staff members to devote time to the planning and organization of all the aspects of the program to be implemented. The philosophical commitment to the broadening of the functions of the psychologist to move away from that of the pure diagnostician to include more of a therapeutic approach, as well as a new concept of preventive functions, bringing in the guidance counselors in an evaluation of courses offered by the school so that the guidance counselors do not serve merely as program planners and schedule makers, bringing in the attendance officer, school nurse, and school social worker with the specialized knowledge and information these people have to offer around particular pupils and their peculiar histories, is a commitment made for the elimination of the inefficiencies in the functioning of individual staff members on the pupil personnel staff and in the school as a whole. The pupil personnel service then, must commit itself to a philosophy which broadens and expands the functions of all the pupil personnel staff members and specifically that of the school psychologist. It must also commit itself to a much closer relationship with the curriculum supervisor for the planning and implementation of the instructional program of the school.

It would seem that confidence in the perceptions and competence of the pupil personnel services would dictate seeking their understanding and cooperation initially, since the basic cooperation to be achieved here is one between pupil personnel and instructional services to which the psychologist and the curriculum supervisor belong respectively. For both specialists not to seek initially the cooperation of the pupil personnel services would indicate either poor perception of those services or a lack of confidence in the capabilities of pupil personnel services to develop the necessary understandings for cooperation in the initial organization of "THE COORDINATED APPROACH."

Less desirable, but still conceivably effective, would be for the curriculum supervisor and psychologist to approach administration first and develop understanding and cooperation from this direction. While in particular instances such an approach might be necessary, involvement of the pupil personnel services after that of the administrative level is bound to be somewhat threatening. However, it is essential that the plunge be taken although a push is often needed.

The reader will see that the attempt that is being made here is to reach the various levels of the school staff simultaneously in developing a true understanding of the meaning of coordination. Administration is approached from one direction, certainly in that administrative support for the implementation of this program is absolutely essential. Pupil personnel is approached from the direction of working within the "middle" school level, in the sense that it is the pupil personnel service which mediates between pupil and faculty. And teachers are approached from a third direction, directly from the pupils themselves.

D. Teacher Understandings for Cooperation

The objective to be achieved here is one of human relations and the development of confidence on the part of teachers in supervisor and psychologist regarding their specialized functions generally, in all of their operations. It would be naive to assume that neither of the two specialists appear as authority figures to teachers. It is the understanding of the need for such authority and what the specialists may contribute to the positive development of teachers, pupils and the all-school program, that must be communicated to teachers by the curriculum supervisor and the psychologist. The object here is to displace the traditional unknown fear of authority and negative value projected on to such specialists by teachers.

Curriculum supervisors and school psychologists, effective even in a traditional setting, must be successful in varying degrees in the development of positive human relationships with teachers to the alleviation of the negative, unenlightened, and perhaps fearful understanding of their authority.

However, even if such relationships are positive, the curriculum supervisor and school psychologist must approach this in developing teacher readiness for involvement in aspects of "THE COORDI-NATED APPROACH." The development of such relationships and understandings must come through the identification of the importance of a preventive approach and of a cooperative enterprise in the all-school program to gain a base of operation. Specific concern must be given to the acceptance of the psychologist as something other than a diagnostician working with disturbed students. Because of the traditional fear of the psychologist as a "head-shrinker," teachers must prepare to understand the objectives and the scope of the school psychologist's involvement in therapeutic and preventive techniques and in analyzing and helping develop new curricula and curricular approaches. This should emphasize the skills and areas of contribution which the psychologist, as an expert in human learning, can bring to such activity. It should help develop confidence among teachers that the psychologist will be primarily viewing and working with them in such activities, **as teachers,** and not as personalities under scrutiny. Failure to gain such acceptance is viewed by the authors to be a critical error. At the same time, the initial contacts and interactions of teachers with the curriculum supervisor and the psychologist should be entered into with strong emphasis upon helping teachers readily see for themselves how involvement of the psychologist in these activities can be of help to them individually and as practitioners in presenting curricula. Out of such positive initial experiences, will come situations in which teachers seek the help of the school psychologist and the subsequent development of a setting in which realistic communications concerning the teacher and his interaction in the all-school program can be discussed with the objective of improved curriculum planning.

The work of the curriculum supervisor and the psychologist at this level can best be facilitated if understandings and cooperation at the administrative and pupil personnel levels have been developed. This will foster a more perceptive understanding and cooperation for the two specialists to work with teachers. It is also conceivable that the psychologist and curriculum supervisor, in developing successful relationships at the teacher level, might be inversely utilized to help the pupil personnel levels and the administration-level readily see the objectives to be gained in "THE COORDINATED APPROACH."

It may be readily agreed by everyone involved that all people working in the school situation, whether in direct contact with pupils or not, need to have a greater understanding of human relationships. Content area is not always primary in the teacher–pupil relationship or in the success gained in teaching the pupil. However, it cannot be easily ignored that teachers who put in a good day's work teaching their youngsters are dog–tired at the end of the day. While the leaders of any teaching group consider what they have to say so important and so valuable that everybody invited should listen, what they are doing is essentially the same thing the teachers do when they are teaching their World History or English Literature or Physics or other subject matter. Teachers, here, are assuming on the basis of their own values and attitudes around the importance of education, that what they have to say is meaningful regardless of how the student happens to feel on that day or regardless of his needs.

All this suggests strongly, and experience confirms, that participation in these programs, whether in–service workshops or teacher consultation or group therapy or classroom visitation, should be entirely voluntary. While we may wish to involve everyone in the school system because of the wonderful things we think we say, we do far better to have only those people attending who are committing themselves to attending because of an interest and motivation which is compatible with what the leaders are trying to do. This makes for much greater communication and far better understanding of what the leaders are trying to impart in their working relationship with the teachers. It is bound also, to further the understanding of the teachers and their relationships with other teachers and pupils. Dependent upon the thoroughness and accuracy of the planning of the program, sufficient interest will be generated throughout the faculty that other members will wish to attend and participate in the activities. While there is much that can be said for requiring attendance of all faculty members in the activities developed within "THE COORDINATED APPROACH", the element of choice would be taken completely away from the teachers. If, however, the program is initiated on a voluntary basis, the experiences gained by the initial participants, if satisfactory, will bring increasing numbers of teachers to the ensuing activities in the program with the personal desire to gain from them.

Again, an operational philosophy must be developed by teachers individually within subject–matter areas, grade levels, and ultimately on a school–wide basis which will help identify the importance of "THE COORDINATED APPROACH," and the greater articulation of the all–school program. Thus, the work of the curriculum supervisor and school psychologist is one of orientation, in–service education, and the development of certain attitudes and understandings. Hopefully, this will result in intelligent cooperation toward developing a functional educational philosophy which will focus upon making operational the cooperative interaction of all of the services of teachers and specialists in the all-school program.

Thus, the tasks for the supervisor and psychologist are identified here as educational in nature and directed toward the development of understanding and cooperation by administration, pupil personnel, and teachers. Therefore, the consideration and organization of "THE COORDINATED APPROACH" must be developed in a setting in which there is a **realistic possibility for this program to be perceived and entered upon** with an intelligent understanding not only of what the program may do, but of some of the problems which must be faced in bringing it to fruition. We may need to start small, but a start must be made!

CHAPTER IV

CONCLUSIONS AND RECOMMENDATIONS

A. Conclusions Drawn from the Experience of Designing and Implementing "THE COORDINATED AP- PROACH"

The designing and implementing of "THE COORDINATED APPROACH" would not have been possible had the authors not carefully scrutinized the instructional and pupil personnel needs of the school system and the implications which this analysis had for their separate areas of function. In examining such needs for these areas of function, the overlapping and omission in services existent in the all–school program became remarkably obvious. If nothing else, the experience of the authors points out that one of the most critical areas of failure in the operation of the American public school is the relatively complete lack of the cooperative examination of the needs of a school system by those responsible for instructional and pupil personnel services. This indicates a definite lack of perception from the point of view that such co-operative analysis of a school situation is infrequent on a broad basis in the spectrum of American public education. Whatever achievements "THE COORDINATED APPROACH" may have had in its implementation at Newfane, it could not have been either designed or implemented without such cooperative study and analysis of special situations as was initially made by the authors. It is not inconceivable that such study, by individual school systems, could result in programs of action based much more upon local and individual needs than those which "THE COORDINATED

APPROACH" can offer. However, it is felt that "THE COORDINATED APPROACH" offers a broad approach for those areas of problem which this text has identified as being long existent because of the lack of coordination between curriculum and school psychological services in our public schools today. If "THE COORDINATED APPROACH" has done nothing else, it has indicated that cooperative planning can best get at these needs of the school system and that these problems must be attacked through a program of cooperative planning which will design and implement activities to involve classroom teaching, the administration, and all the special services of the school. Failure to do so, would seem to indicate perpetuate the inefficiency in function existent in the American public school with its present isolation of special services, particularly those of the curriculum supervisor and the school psychologist.

Thus, the authors consider the paramount need of the American public school system to be one of the development of a realistic and total commitment to the articulation of the school system and the organization of a program in which the cooperative consideration of the educational needs of students and the community will be undertaken, not through the isolation of staff positions, but through the bringing together of the various points of view and skills which these specialists have in the planning of an approach which would utilize the skills of every member of the professional staff to his optimal effectiveness. If "THE COORDINATED APPROACH" indicates nothing else, it indicates that this optimal effectiveness cannot be identified through isolated analysis and isolated attack upon that aspect of the all–school program with which that area of specialization happens to be responsible and skilled. Thus, if not "THE COORDINATED APPROACH," the American public school needs "A COORDINATED APPROACH" which has never become actually operational. The programs, techniques, and methods which are developed in "THE COORDINATED APPROACH" will be of greatest value if all the specialists and the faculty involved in the all–school program have been oriented to operate **professionally in a setting which understands and encourages communication and cooperation within the total school setting.** The team–approach can work only when the need and advantages are seen and ultimately felt by all people involved in the situation at–large. It is felt by the authors, that a significant achievement of the designing and implementing of "THE COORDINATED APPROACH" was the development of the awareness of the need for a greater team–approach involving all of the specialists in the school setting as well as the faculty. The activities developed in "THE COORDINATED APPROACH" attempted to make clear and important the need for such teamwork. The identification and development of attitudes and understandings for the importance of coordination in the all-school program was a central objective of activities such as the teacher group therapy programs and the elementary and secondary school review workshops. In the planning of units and the operation of the authors as consultants in the classroom, the functional advantages of utilizing the special skills of all members of the professional staff were operationalized. As a result of these activities, the teachers engaged actively in a program of inter-classroom visitation. In most instances this is now handled by the teachers themselves with the involvement of a curriculum supervisor and the administration only where help is needed in covering a class or classes so that this program may be extended.

This program is basically the visitation of classes by other teachers who are teaching in the same subject-matter area and/or grade level. Teachers have found this to be an excellent opportunity to improve their own backgrounds in terms of identifying new instructional techniques and new and different approaches to similar problems and curricular programs. Because there is no evaluative implication, it is assumed by the authors, due to their experiences in the activities of "THE COORDINATED APPROACH," that insecurity of individual teachers has been reduced to a minimum. The wholehearted enthusiasm of teachers who have had growing experiences in such activity has encouraged others to become involved. This has also resulted in an informalized team-approach wherein teachers who have a particular skill in a given area have gone into other classes as guests or visiting experts. The most sophisticated experiences developed through this activity have been teacher panels, meeting before several classes at a time, and in the case of the English department, readings of drama to be performed before several classes at a time in the school auditorium. In other instances, teachers have taped such an activity for its use in other class settings or in subsequent years.

Underlying this is the basic assumption that the faculty is at all times professional. If a teacher is threatened by visitation or exchange, and she finds sharing and coordination an experience she prefers to avoid, then she needs help to realize how she sabotages more effective learning. This is often a most challenging task and a discouraging one. But for coordination to be more than a word on paper, such an aversion must be avoided at all costs.

The authors conclude that "THE COORDINATED APPROACH" has achieved the following areas of growth in its initial implementation. First, a coordinated examination of the needs of the school evolved with study and analysis of such problems being taken on cooperatively by the specialized areas of the staff through the focus of the instructional and pupil personnel services. A value has been placed on such a cooperative approach which, it is felt, will insure a more realistic understanding of the needs for the articulation of all of the services of the school which never would have been possible had such special services continued to operate in an atmosphere of isolation, which is so typical throughout American public education. In addition, cooperative self-evaluation has greater value for the local situation than when such evaluation comes from an outside and often remote agent such as state education offices.

Second, understanding and enthusiasm has developed over the desire to build a coordinated team-approach in the operationalization of the all-school program. The experiences of teachers gained through aspects of "THE COORDINATED APPROACH" has provided teachers with a new and personally meaningful experience which has instilled confidence in the values of the team-approach. This has resulted in a clearer insight by teachers into instructional and curricular problems and their willingness to utilize services of the curriculum supervisor and the pupil personnel services, particularly the school psychologist, for greater effectiveness than ever before.

A third area of achievement was the development of attitudes and the change in some previous attitudes regarding the interaction of teachers with their colleagues. The interaction among teachers in planning and identifying approaches to specific instructional problems has indicated further acceptance of the importance of the team-approach. The development of inter-classroom visitation and the utilization of teachers as visiting experts, panelists, etc., has made for broader effectiveness in the instructional program. Similarly, teachers now place extremely little value on the isolation of themselves from their colleagues and they are more interested in sharing ideas rather than carefully guarding ideas, techniques, and materials which they have developed themselves.

B. Recommendations for Expanding the Depth and Scope of "THE COORDINATED APPROACH" for General Application in Public School Systems

The authors have contended that "THE COORDINATED APPROACH" may serve to meet the needs of different school systems serving different kinds of pupils. Similarly, the authors have contended that the implementation of "THE COORDINATED APPROACH" could be facilitated by any school system having the services of a curriculum supervisor and a school psychologist and would result in no outlay of funds at such an initial level. As has been indicated, the commitment which is needed for the implementation of "THE COORDINATED APPROACH" is a philosophical one with the necessary implication for leadership and support in moving toward the objectives of "THE COORDINATED APPROACH!"

Chapter III of the text has identified what it is felt constitutes the broad requirements for "THE COORDINATED APPROACH." Within the setting at Newfane, the leadership was provided by the curriculum supervisor and the school psychologist, and the necessary understandings of the administration were identified. In considering the extension of the concept of "THE COORDINATED APPROACH," necessary leadership roles cannot be obviated. This may come initially from the curriculum supervisor and/or the school psychologist or from either pupil personnel services or the administration. However, the task for leadership and the presentation of the implications of "THE COORDINATED APPROACH" for that particular school setting is a task, the importance of which becomes quite obvious. It must also be readily recognized that an interest in implementing "THE COORDINATED APPROACH" also is an admission of particular areas of need in the school which point to something less than a desired level of articulation or coordination in the planning of the all-school program and the orientation of teachers toward the team approach. Hence, the most important element here may be recognition of a situation of lack with regard to the areas of improvement which "THE COORDINATED APPROACH" maintains it can facilitate.

At the same time the authors see additional conditions which should be sought after for more effective expansion of the depth and scope of "THE COORDINATED APPROACH." These would have to do primarily with the area of authority delegated to the positions of the curriculum supervisor and the school psychologist. The authors recommend that if "THE COORDINATED APPROACH" is to be implemented in a given school system that the curriculum supervisor and the school psychologist be delegated authority to operate with responsibility on a system-wide basis throughout the elementary and secondary school programs. Where there are more than one of each of these specialists, a division of schools will be necessary, but the commitment is system-wide.

At the same time, the authors cannot stress too much the importance of developing confidence by the faculty in their respective roles as specialists to the point of dispelling threat in looking toward "THE COORDINATED APPROACH." Failure to proceed slowly and develop confidence in a sound, human relations rapport may cause not only the curriculum supervisor and the school psychologist but all the implications of "THE COORDINATED APPROACH" to bring extreme hazards to the emotional security of teachers. While the prospects of such change may be encouraging and challenging to some teachers, it will be threatening to others. The promulgation of "THE COORDINATED APPROACH" must not be vague or poorly defined since this will present even more of a threat than a specific identification of what the program is and what it seeks to do. It would be unrealistic to expect that teachers concerned with their own professional responsibilities will have a real enthusiasm for the program unless the real advantages to them and for the program of the school can be clearly explicated. The tasks of the leaders in implementing "THE COORDINATED APPROACH" will be to appeal to the sense of idealism and professional responsibility of teachers so that it overcomes some of the negative possibilities which the changes implied by the program may suggest.

This means that the validity and the rationale for the program should be understood by the faculty so that the program may be evaluated rather than uncritically accepted or rejected. The introduction of this program can best be accomplished in a situation where teachers have come to expect that curriculum planning is part of a regular, on-going activity in the school and where teachers are accustomed to a development and change of program as needs become identifiable and solutions practical.

Where such conditions are not present, it would seem most logical to first orient the faculty to the importance of curriculum planning and the identification of how curriculum planning activities should be a part of a regular on-going program of continuous evaluation and improvement of the all-school program. Similarly, it must be recognized that "THE COORDINATED APPROACH" cannot be piled on teachers in addition to their regular work.

"THE COORDINATED APPROACH" is designed to enhance the effectiveness of the all-school program through developing a preventive approach and a perceptive awareness on the part of teachers, as well as understandings which they will take into the operational settings of their classrooms. To this end, the authors contend that the school should be concerned with providing conditions and incentives for teachers to participate in the various aspects of the program. This would include possibility of release time opportunity and the compensation of in-service education credit toward the salary barriers of the school system for teachers who participated in the Workshops. After all, if the school system or the school, seeking to implement "THE COORDINATED APPROACH," is not willing to invest something or to put simple recognition upon the program and participation in it, it does not seem fair to expect a teacher to make this solely out of professional enthusiasm or idealism.

The authors strongly maintain that this program can sell itself on its merits, but that compulsory involvement under the aegis of the school administration will doom it to something less than the success which it might otherwise enjoy. It is true that the teachers who will, in all probability, be in the greatest need of participation in aspects of the program will not be those who will initially seek out participation. It is maintained, however, that initial satisfaction on the part of the first participants in aspects of the program, will create an interest on the part of other faculty members. If the experience of the first participants can help them to perceive and operate more effectively in terms of instructional problems and problems with students, other teachers will be interested in participating. It has been the experience of the authors that the interest of teachers in various of the aspects of "THE COORDINATED APPROACH" grew algebraically as teachers who were involved in the activities became enthusiastic about their experience in the program and the immediate benefits which they could apply to their classroom teaching situations.

The teacher must have the opportunity to elect or not to elect his participation in such activities. Not to do so, will introduce a threat to the emotional security of the teacher and any feeling of being compelled to participate would invariably bring him to these experiences with a negative attitude. It is felt that "THE COORDINATED APPROACH" will not bring group pressure upon the teacher to participate and that the nature of the Review Workshops and the Teacher-Group-Therapy have been designed to carefully introspect the importance of human relations and of the dangers of group pressure or domination of the individual. In addition to the perceptions already mentioned, it is hoped that participants in the program will be more understanding of their relationships with colleagues in terms of recognizing the individual differences of teachers with whom they work. Optimally, participants in the program would operate more discretely with teachers making an attempt to take into account the particular kinds of skills and backgrounds of their colleagues and differences which they may have as individual persons.

It goes without saying that the leadership to move toward implementing "THE COORDINATED APPROACH" comes from the administration although the curriculum supervisor and school psychologist may bring the idea to administration. But it is absolutely critical that administration give the program impetus through its support and encouragement. And it is equally critical to its success

that the curriculum supervisor and school psychologist wholeheartedly endorse it before they attempt to implement it. It would seem
obvious that the commitment to such a program must come from
those who assume its leadership and direction. As was noted earlier,
if the school administration and especially those administrators
closest to the teachers--building principals--accept the philosophy
presented here, they can take giant steps towards alleviating the
threat faculty so often feels at the introduction of something a little
newer or a little different.

The coordination stressed here has focused on that primarily
involving the curriculum supervisor and the school psychologist. There
is no reason why this kind of coordinated effort could not operate
in many different areas. It is probable that there are at least as
many different coordinating combinations within the schools as there
are personnel trained in the different areas of function. Thus, it is
possible to arrange coordinating combinations of teaching specialties
with each other (as, for example, in team teaching or as a second
example, in the development of basic library materials utilizing
different levels of reading ability combined with different interest
levels). It is possible to coordinate teaching specialties with the non-
teaching professional staff (as, for example, in the development of
an all school health program so that the nurses' teaching skills be
utilized fully beginning at the earliest levels to inculcate the knowledge and spirit of good health habits). Whatever the combinations,
they should have the common objective of the development of a more
efficient functioning educational setting where in truth, the whole
is more than a sum of its component parts.

An area of coordination which is vital to the smooth functioning
of the American school and which has been relatively untapped,
involves coordination between school and parents. P.T.A. does not
serve the function of coordination demanded because too often the
P.T.A. program is quite unrelated to the needs of the school, but
is one which rather fills the needs of the select parents who participate in P.T.A.

One of the most frequent cooperative ventures involving parent-
child–teacher relationships is the one in which parents are asked to
or for other reasons assume the responsibility of helping their children with homework. It is well known that this often confuses the
caught–in–the–middle child because parents teach quite differently
than teachers! And it is equally well known that the rapid changes
in education with the problems of programmed teaching, the ungraded class, variations in report cards and marking systems, such
course problems as those raised by modern math, to name a few,
leave parents quite confused and resentful when their youngsters run
into academic difficulties. The innovation of "Modern Mathematics"

and its acceptance in the curriculum of the contemporary elementary and secondary school poses a threat to many parents. This is a unique situation for the average parent accustomed to helping his child with homework. One of the most difficult things for too many parents to admit is that they are not knowledgeable in certain areas, and the new math has rendered mathematical understandings of the average parent obsolete. Even the primary student taking his orientation to modern math now knows more about something new than his parent could have ever experienced, even if he were a proficient "old" math student. The parent must now admit his lack of omnipotence and recognize this obsolescence. While it is acceptable and comfortable for the parent to acknowledge this and relinquish this when his child begins advanced training beyond high school, it's a tremendous demoralizer to his ego when his six-year old poses this threat.

Obviously, the scope of coordination may be broadened in many directions. All that is really necessary, is a commitment to the philosophy of coordination. The authors contend that much of the hostility directed at education today will be alleviated by this approach. Isolationism proved a folly many years ago.

C. Implications of "THE COORDINATED APPROACH" for the Education of Teachers, Curriculum Supervisors, and School Psychologists

As a result of the experiences of the authors with "THE CO-ORDINATED APPROACH" certain implications have become evident for the education of teachers, curriculum supervisors, and school psychologists. Both authors have had considerable experience in the field of teacher education, and have perceived some of the problems which occur in the education of teachers. In addition, they have seen first hand the kinds of "in-practice" problems which can result from certain gaps in teacher education. Experiencing then, what is essentially seen from at least two points of view, pre-service and in-service operational settings, they conclude that much of what serves as objectives in "THE COORDINATED APPROACH" similarly should serve as objectives for pre-service as well as graduate teacher education.

As this text has strongly suggested, much of the ineffectiveness of the American public school evolves from the vacuum in which such education takes place. Throughout, the authors have stressed that subject matter which has no meaning for the experiencing students is sterile and devoid of significance. Therefore, teacher education should be critically concerned with the effective preparation of prospective teachers so that they will be able to perceptively and effectively teach their subject matter to students. At the same time these prospective teachers are expected to be prepared to identify and meet the needs of individuals within a class and be aware of the characteristics and problems which may be expected from that particular age group. The failure of so many teachers to perform with such awarenesses and skills indicates that what has been provided in teacher education has not been sufficient, realistic, or meaningful for a large number of teacher education students. A striking example of this kind of subject matter taught to freshmen education students is seen in courses in child development and educational psychology. It is expected by conscientious educators of teachers that this subject area provides the teacher-to-be with information and understandings which she will never forget and which will cause her to be sensitively aware and perceptive of the individual student and his needs. It is a gross error of judgment to assume that such a course or courses, offered at a time when freshmen students have not yet themselves moved very far from childhood and adolescence, is a meaningful experience. Many of these same students are too much engrossed with themselves as recently emancipated from home, or in the process of bridging the gap between dependence and independence, to view such material with a sensitive insight into others. They are still too concerned with themselves. Unfortunately, many of these same students will complete their undergraduate teacher preparation without again encountering any formal course work in child development and educational psychology.

It is not the intention of the authors to point out how such vitally important material should be introduced to the student so that it has meaningful significance in the concrete practice of teaching. It is the intention of the authors, however, to point out that the sterile techniques lamented in the public school are also lamentable at the college level. "THE COORDINATED APPROACH" maintains that the learnings of any educational experience are most effective and permanent when they are organized within a Gestalt which seeks to identify the needs and interests of individuals and relate what is to be learned to them. How can it ever be hoped to accomplish this at the one level of education without demanding it at the other?

The authors agree that experience in teacher education and the problems which many teachers encounter in their teaching should necessitate a conscientious review of the objectives of undergraduate teacher education as well as those means by which teacher education curricula seeks to achieve these objectives. It would seem that the objectives of contemporary teacher education would be reinforced as they presently exist, but that curricular programs in teacher education must become realistically concerned with making the experiences of prospective teachers much more meaningful and realistic. Such a reorganization of teacher education, it is hoped, would provide beginning teachers with awarenesses, understandings, and personal commitments as well as skills so as to equip them to organize the learning situation in their classroom to be more meaningful. In addition, and with growing significance, it would help inculcate within the prospective teacher an incentive for individual study and thinking which will result in tremendous personal reward and greater professional effectiveness. What is there in teacher education that instills this incentive now?

Most educators will agree that some place in teacher preparation should be reserved for the study of human relations. The authors will certainly agree that human relations is an area of critical importance in teacher education and the operational setting of the public school. However, the authors violently disagree with any thinking which claims that human relations is a course or that it can be learned from textbooks, no matter how well written. Human relations is an experience and for effective learning to occur, it must be felt in the context of human interaction.

The effectiveness of a teaching situation is critically dependent upon the teacher's interaction with his pupils. It should follow that when the teacher has a growing awareness of himself as an individual with feelings and hopes and pains and prejudices, that his interaction with his pupils should improve. Such an awareness cannot be developed in a typical classroom experience in an academic setting which relies upon the mastery of textbooks and other instructional materials. It may possibly be developed through a laboratory setting or seminar situation in which a skilled teacher works with a small class of students. However, the probability of developing such awarenesses for all students in even this seminar or laboratory setting is not encouraging.

The authors submit that one of the most effective activities of "THE COORDINATED APPROACH" would have broad and deep implications for teacher education in the development of the kinds of personal awarenesses involved in human interaction. This activity is group therapy.

It is a strange twist of fate that permits a relatively young, naive and inexperienced teacher to enter into a classroom and influence a group of twenty or thirty students academically, emotionally, and socially. Such influence may not be devastating but it is bound to be something less than optimal in terms of the encouragement of learning and the positive catalytic influence it might have on the development of students. What worth would the teacher have who nurtures growth and excites learning through his awareness of the process of human relations?

The authors are convinced that a reasonably realistic self-appraisal is essential to good teaching. This means that the teacher is aware not only of his assets but of his liabilities and that in this awareness he is willing to assume responsibility for developing his skills to the fullest potential. It also means that he will not hide behind various excuses which detract from his skills as a teacher and as an honest human being. It means that he will become more a self-respecting person and less a defensive person struggling for the romance of professionalism.

Group therapy is not a panacea and it is not suggested here that all the personal problems and inadequacies of the prospective teacher can be eliminated or alleviated through this experience. It does, however, offer a valuable opportunity to examine one's motives and aspirations in seeking a career in education. That is one essential examination. Dissatisfaction in a teaching career does not contribute to good teaching. Furthermore, too many teacher education students choose teaching as a field because it offers security, a college degree, and does not cost much. Others choose teaching because they cannot succeed in programs leading to other occupational or professional qualification. While initial motivation for entry into teaching as a career is no guarantee of success or failure as a teacher, understandings of the kind that may be encouraged through group therapy can help the prospective teacher to achieve a more realistic self-appraisal and a more comfortable compromise, if one is necessary.

It may seem from the above discussion that group therapy is directed solely toward developing understanding of the personal motivations involved in entering teaching. Certainly, this is one objective that may be sought after. However, through supportive self-examination, as may reasonably take place in group therapy, recognition and airing of one's feelings towards children with varied backgrounds and values, of one's fears of failure as a person as well as teacher, and one's chance to observe the give and take of a communicating process can afford the prospective teacher not only considerable insight into himself, but can help him build sensitivity and compassion in his relationships with others. The authoritative leadership of the teacher may be a source of primary satisfaction to the prospective teacher because of his need to use his strength to manipulate people rather than to lead them. Realizing this kind of need and understanding the dynamics underlying it, can save many youngsters much discomfort.

While such an activity would be a radical departure from present teacher education, the authors maintain that the critical need to develop personally meaningful and effective human relations awareness in teachers merits the consideration of therapy as an effective means to this end. The experience of "THE COORDINATED APPROACH" has seen the effectiveness of such therapy in developing such awarenesses for teachers within their school setting. Similar accomplishments could be expected of group therapy experiences for undergraduate teacher education students. If the kinds and degrees of awarenesses developed by group therapy for teachers in the school setting with "THE COORDINATED APPROACH" could be developed in undergraduate teacher education, the preparedness of beginning teachers to operate with a preventive approach to human relations in the classroom would be a staggering advancement over what such preparedness is now.

"THE COORDINATED APPROACH" has identified the need for greater integration of the educational experiences of the American public school. This integration should seek to bring the learnings in subject-matter areas into a focus which interrelates with the needs, interests, and experiences of the individual student within the reality of his environmental context. The authors have decried the relative ineffectiveness and lack of permanence of much of what the public school teaches because it is taught in isolation from such experiences of students. This point is repeatedly made in this text.

Similarly the curricula and total experience of undergraduate teacher education should provide such an integrated focus for the prospective teacher. Failure to systematically plan a closely interrelated program of teacher education at this level causes much of the program experienced by the prospective teacher to remain isolated from the important focus of providing him with adequate preparation in terms of skills, understandings, awarenesses, and perceptions to begin his teaching. While many of the experiences provided the pre-service teacher education student are of excellent worth in themselves, they cannot contribute optimally to the preparation of the teacher unless they are related to the total program of teacher education through salient and effective curriculum planning. Students in teacher education as well as elementary and secondary school students will not develop a broad background of facts, skills, understandings, and awarenesses unless the total curricular experience which they will undergo is planned to help facilitate the achievement of these objectives. Thus at the teacher education level as well as at all other levels of education, it is unrealistic to expect that students will be able to achieve their maximum potential for learning and development unless the program at-large is planned to facilitate this, by providing a context of meaning and goal-value for the student.

The depth, breadth, and scope of student teaching as the culminating experience in teacher education is one of inconsistent extremes if viewed at a regional or national level. In some situations student teaching is part of junior year experience and in others is offered only in the senior year prior to completion of the teacher education curriculum. In some instances student teaching requires a full year with one situation. In others a semester suffices while in still others two half semester experiences are required. Some broad agreement as to the objectives of these programs should result in a commitment to a program of a particular scope. There seems to be merit in spending an entire year with classes. Similarly there is value to spending time in more than one situation to compare them and the student teacher's growth in separate experiences. Certainly, research into the effectiveness of the varied types of experiences and the strengths and weaknesses of each in preparing for teaching is in order.

Of great importance in each of the varied approaches to student teaching is the manner in which this experience is planned to meet the total objectives of the teacher education program. It should build carefully upon the earlier preparation of prospective teachers through their academic experience and observation of and participation in educational situations. Student teachers should be thoroughly prepared to meet the demands of their student teaching placement in terms of the school, community, and the kinds of children they will meet there. Similarly, the nature of their supervision in student teaching and the relation of seminars and classes taken on their campuses before, during, and immediately following their student teaching has a tremendous responsibility to help them gain maximum benefit from student teaching. Such experiences should help the student teacher to coordinate and pull together his previous experiences in child growth and development, sociology, teaching methods courses and what his observation and participation experience may have provided him as a resource for student teaching. These are the experiences which teacher education programs most generally fail to coordinate and pull into focus for student teachers. Coordination at this level is seen as a critical need in helping student teachers develop awarenesses, understandings, and perceptively utilize their background of skills, facts, and information to prepare them as effectively as possible to gain from student teaching as much as they can prior to their moving into their own relatively independent teaching situations upon graduation. In reflecting upon the needs of beginning and experienced teachers through the experiences of "THE COORDINATED APPROACH," the authors view this common lack of coordination and curricular planning in teacher education to be the cause of considerable classroom myopia if not blindness.

Internship is an established practice in many vocational and professional areas. However, public schools and teacher education have never broadly considered the possibilities of internship before entrance into full-time teaching service. This has partially been due to periods of shortage of teachers but historically the need for teacher internship has never been broadly contemplated. Student teaching has given various degrees of exposure and preparation for teachers but this has been done as a part of teacher education and has seldom provided the student teacher with the broad range of responsibilities which he will encounter in his first teaching situation. The authors submit that the experiences with teachers in "THE CO-ORDINATED APPROACH" and the range of problems faced by student teachers, as just described, and by first year teachers have strong implications for a period of internship for beginning teachers, following their student teaching and graduation from teacher education programs.

Such internship would effectively be implemented through an experience of part or half-time employment of teachers in a public school situation. This internship experience could be effectively complemented by a balanced half or part-time program of beginning graduate or in-service education. Such internship would require strong supervision by experienced curriculum personnel who would be responsible for organizing the in-service or graduate study part of the experience. This would allow for either the school system or a teacher education institution to be involved in the educative aspect of the program. Certainly "THE COORDINATED APPROACH" could be programmed for such interns within a particular public school setting for an in-service education program. This would seek to coordinate the problems of teaching interns with the bodies of knowledge and the emerging awarenesses, understandings, and perceptions upon which "THE COORDINATED APPROACH" has been based.

Upon completion of this year of internship these teachers would assume full-time teaching positions with what the authors contend would be much greater chances for success in teaching and a significantly greater degree of skill and preparedness from that which existent student teaching alone can provide. Also it is felt that many individuals having strong potential for teaching who leave teaching after an unpleasant first year experience might remain in teaching and make effective contributions were such internship programs operational. At the same time an internship experience might help individuals not really interested in teaching or who are not capable of becoming successful teachers not to pursue the area any further. Unfortunately such an approach to internship for teaching has received practically no thought from educators and this concept will require widespread promulgation and consideration. An interesting attempt in this direction has been the Inter-University Project One, supported by the Ford Foundation. This unique program in teacher education has been implemented in New York State on the campuses of the State University of New York at Buffalo, Cornell University, the University of Rochester, and Syracuse University. This program sought the identification of candidates for the project from teacher education students in their freshman and sophomore years. Students selected were put into a highly coordinated and integrated teacher education program which culminated in student teaching experiences in teaching center schools, selected and developed by the project to represent various communities and social strata. Critic teachers in these teaching center schools were given intensive in-service education experiences to prepare them for their roles. Upon graduation, internships were provided for some of the graduates on a half-time employment on regular faculty basis and a half-time graduate and in-service education basis designed to refine the experiences of the internship. The authors conclude that the general approach of Project One and its implementation of an internship program could mark a program of great implications for the effective entrance of teachers into their teaching service. (The program is explained in detail by publications of the project itself.[1])

That something of this sort is crucial to teacher training is clear as far as the authors are concerned. The panic with which the beginning teacher often becomes involved and to which so many surrender is without doubt closely related to the level of security he brings to his teaching situation. This security can be strengthened in at least the two ways mentioned here, i.e., group therapy and a more interrelated and coordinated-with-experience teacher training program. Through the former situation, anxieties arising from dependency needs and inexperience can be markedly alleviated while the training process continues. Through the latter kind of training and the internship, the realistic dread of jumping into an independent teaching situation without reasonable experience, is made unnecessary because reasonable experience will have been had.

Lest the reader raise an eyebrow because this in-service-in-training kind of program is costly to develop and time-consuming, let him be aware that the frightened first year teacher practices

[1]**Focusing Teacher Preparation in Teaching Center Schools,** Inter-University Project One, Supported by the Ford Foundation: State University of New York at Buffalo, Buffalo, New York, 1965.

without the threat of killing his patients (as might be the case with the brand new physician) but there is considerable possibility of maiming a goodly number of his charges.

The area of graduate professional teacher education also seems to suffer from the problems of isolation. The authors contend that the range and scope of graduate teacher education could become markedly more realistic and meaningful to the needs of teachers were course offerings to be more closely developed concerning the problems and needs of teachers as they manifest themselves within schools. While existing course offerings do provide many essential areas of information, in many instances they have not kept pace with the impact of characteristics of contemporary society as they manifest themselves to classroom teachers through the students who come to the public school. The authors do not intend to include in this category those graduate education offerings for areas such as guidance, administration, and curriculum development. The concern here is for courses which are offered for teachers seeking additional educational experience and advanced training to improve their effectiveness as teachers. Likewise, the programs leading to graduate degrees for teachers should include courses which would focus upon emerging problems in classrooms and evolving concepts and techniques of instruction which would advance the skills, awarenesses, and perceptions of teachers. The authors' experiences in "THE COORDINATED APPROACH" lead them to conclude that the areas included in the Elementary and Secondary Review Workshops, as described in Chapter II, constitute important areas for the development of salient graduate offerings for teachers. This may mean that the graduate programs of teacher education institutions should consider providing more extension course experiences to be taken by graduate school instructors into the context of particular schools and school systems. The areas of graduate course offerings can thereby be brought into the focus of the needs of a particular faculty reflecting the needs of the individual community served by that school. It is felt that the Elementary and Secondary Workshops of "THE COORDINATED APPROACH" will help individual schools and school systems to develop awarenesses leading to their demand to teacher education campuses to provide more extension course to meet the needs of their particular faculties. This means, of course, that schools of education can no longer remain in isolation either!

These ramifications for the development of graduate education offerings and the increased organization of these into extension courses should similarly bring more attention to the general need for in-service education throughout the American public school. Individual schools and school systems could achieve greater effectiveness if the practice of continuous in-service education programs was developed to bear upon the emerging needs of teachers, the curriculum, and the all-school program. It is here that the impact of the Elementary and Secondary Review Workshops of "**THE CO-ORDINATED APPROACH**" may help develop important insights. The areas considered as outlined in that section of the text could serve to review and focus on important needs of teachers in almost all elementary and secondary school classrooms. The awarenesses which the Workshops seek to develop should lead a faculty to further consider its needs as teachers, departments, and grade levels and as school units. If the teachers perceive this initial in-service education experience of the Review Workshops to have been of practical and real value in their teaching, their interest in further in-service and their expectation of its value should be high. If a continuous program of in-service education is seized upon, teachers may make increasingly effective choices of personal graduate education experience, demands for extension courses to be brought into their schools, and in-service programs to be organized to meet evolving teacher and curricular needs.

Still another implication of "**THE COORDINATED APPROACH**" for teacher training lies in the growing complexity of pupil evaluation. American public schools have traversed the extremes in evaluating their pupils. Colleges dealing with admission concerns have needed to rely heavily on techniques other than teacher grades in order to establish some standardized achievement measure by which to determine college aptitude. In view, too, of the heavy reliance on teacher evaluation for the determination of homogeneous groupings and educational tracks, teacher evaluation has obviously tremendous import.

Yet, what is the validity of teacher judgment generally when pupil evaluation is the problem? What does it mean in the ungraded classroom, or in the A–B–C system, or the S and U grading procedure, or in the numbers game? What does it mean when a child is compared "with himself" as well as with his peers? Finally, what does teacher evaluation do to the child himself, and to the reality of his self-perceptions and the perceptions others have of him?

Aside from the obvious need for mandatory training in tests and measurements in the academic sequence as well as in the internship and student teaching setting, there should be provision for serious study of the development of evaluation anxiety, an anxiety experienced at all levels K through 12 and to no one's surprise, among teachers.

The psychologist in the school setting is invariably requested to evaluate the ability of children on the basis that such children are underachievers, slow learners, or retarded. It is unlikely that any school psychologist working in a typical public school has not experienced some concern at finding the "under-achiever" is really retarded or a slow learner, concern because it means that the teacher's evaluational judgment of that child is in error, or the child is not a slow learner, but a serious underachiever. It is an amazing concern because so many teachers cannot make an adequate evaluation because they do not know the difference.

This is not unrelated to the common situation of the teacher who is a "hard marker" or its opposite, or of the teacher who has impossible expectations, or who evaluates progress in reading on the basis of his liking the child or his hygiene. That these situations exist serves as testimony to the need for considerably more realistic and meaningful study of test making and test taking. Even the Kindergarten pupil bears his report card home with pride when he sees the S's and the I's more frequent that the N's.

Among the strongest implications of "THE COORDINATED APPROACH" are those ramifications for the education of curriculum supervisors and school psychologists. As this approach has been described in the text, it is these specialists who must provide the leadership in orienting, designing, and implementing the program. The necessary skills that the authors have found to be valuable in their own activities have developed from the perceptions gained in working together and some which they brought to their original joint association. Thus, the background of professional education and special training which brings a person to operate in either one of these two specialist's roles must necessarily allow the individual to develop important attitudes, awarenesses, and perceptions of the nature of his tasks, as well as specific skills to take action as he faces the problems in his professional operational setting.

An important initial problem which, from many points of view, may be the most critical, is the amount of isolation which advanced training can develop. Until relatively recently, these areas of specialty have been communicative only with other members of the same areas. It is only now that the need for general orientation in broad fields is gaining support in the planning of advanced programs for the training of educational specialists.

The curriculum supervisor comes to his position from many different orientations and in some instances suffers from being too much the generalist and in others too much the specialist. In many cases, the school administrator has also been delegated responsibilities for curriculum development which he has had to discharge himself. Regardless of such a person's abilities to operate in the field of curriculum planning, the administrative hat and club which he is perceived to hold by faculty members, is bound to negate his chances of optimal success as a curriculum planner. As was noted in Chapter II, the tasks of supervisor and curriculum consultant are more easily combined, but the individual must not be delegated any hard administrative responsibility or else his ability to operate as a consultant with teachers will be impaired. The concept of the curriculum supervisor as a consultant and coordinator rather than a supervisor or administrator is one which is growing in acceptance and which is, in many areas of the country, becoming a recognized position and one with which teachers are becoming familiar. The education of such a person and his qualifications to accept such a position are of critical importance, but even more so, if he is to be knowledgeable and effective in working in cooperation with a school psychologist in any aspects of the approach which this text has sought to explicate.

In many instances curriculum supervisors have been in-bred from their teaching faculty in terms of their experience alone. It may be that with a highly perceptive individual this is an excellent credential. However, specific training is required in terms of the skills of curriculum planning, human relations, methods and techniques of instruction, and related instructional media. Such training is most frequently offered at the post–masters degree level. This is commendable and it is this level of education which can effectively build upon and take advantage of an individual's perceptions, experience in undergraduate teacher education, teaching experience, and graduate education to the master's degree.

While it will be identified that it is not deemed necessary for the school psychologist it is highly important that the curriculum supervisor be an experienced teacher and one who is perceptive of the broad problems of instruction. His involvement in graduate training in terms of curriculum planning, human relations, techniques of instruction and related media of instruction can be most effective only if he has a background of his own perceptions and reflections upon his experience as a teacher.

While not explicitly stated in most programs of professional education for curriculum supervisors, there is an implied need for training in the skills of group dynamics, psychology of the child, adolescent and the adult, and a basic working knowledge of psychodynamics with particular reference to group therapy. Basic exposure to counselling techniques also seem important in terms of the amount of working and, in a real sense, counselling, which the specialist will do with teachers on a one–to–one basis. Of course, failure to have a strong orientation and experience in the area of human relations will doom the curriculum supervisor to innumerable failures despite his other strong skills and whatever perceptive awarenesses his advanced training may develop.

Traditionally, the types of experiences which have been identified here are not part of the typical orientation and professional education of the curriculum supervisor. We are still at a point where the availability of such trained specialists is far exceeded by the growing demand for curriculum supervisors in the public school setting. It is this which has been a strong contributing factor to the substitution of people with various kinds of training, no training, and mere familiarity or experience in teaching in that particular school system. Such situations have not been exclusively negative in which people of perception have sought advanced professional training to supplement their experience and have become skillful in fulfilling the demands of the curriculum supervisor's position. Of considerable incidence, however, are situations in which the position of curriculum supervisor has become an administrative one or one of strictly a supervisory and evaluative function concerned with the hiring and firing of teachers. Too often, such positions have never become concerned with helping beginning teachers or experienced teachers with problems, and work for the solution of their problems. To do this, the kinds of training which have been indicated in the areas of instructional techniques, related media of instruction, instructional materials, and the experience of successful teaching by the supervisor should properly come into play. Unfortunately, too many of these situations can be seen to project that the teacher will either improve on his own or from the suggestions of other teachers with whom he may have the confidence to associate. In such situations the school has failed in its responsibility to help the teacher develop his skills to the point of rendering satisfactory or commendable service.

The types of activities which "THE COORDINATED APPROACH" has focused upon have been designed to help the teachers do this. Since many of the problems faced by the teacher in the classroom relate to those problems of the student in his adjustment to the school, it is felt by the authors that close cooperation between the instructional and pupil personnel services especially, through the tasks of the curriculum supervisor and the school psychologist, is necessary beyond the limits which the average school situation with its lack of articulation of these services, has offered.

Thus, the most critical area of need of the curriculum supervisor is in the area of awarenesses. Such lack of the awareness of the importance of the need for cooperation between instructional and pupil personnel services is most frequently found where the specialist has come to his position through inbreeding and without benefit of specialized training. The mere excellence or effectiveness of a teacher should not be sufficient to qualify him for a position as a curriculum supervisor. Even for those persons with advanced training in the areas of curriculum planning, instructional techniques, related instructional media and human relations, the overview of the awareness of the importance for the articulation and cooperative planning between the instructional and pupil personnel services may not have developed. The experience of the authors in designing and implementing "THE COORDINATED APPROACH" indicates that the advanced training of the curriculum supervisor should take on a very special focus. This focus should seek to identify not only the importance of the articulation of these areas within the public school setting, but the development of channels for communication and techniques that will allow understandings to develop between these two areas in the public school system and, hopefully, cooperative planning. If there is a focal point of weakness in the developing of the instructional aspects of the all–school program, it is that the consideration of the instructional program and its growth and development has operated largely in isolation, and therefore an atomosphere in which awareness of the importance of the knowledge of the pupil and his problems has not been created to establish its focus upon prevention in a curriculum design. This has, unfortunately, been relegated to the pupil personnel area, with the responsibilities for diagnosis and therapy directed toward the tasks of the counselors and school psychologists. Even where this therapeutic course has taken place, there has been relatively no contact between the curriculum supervisor and the specialists within the area of pupil personnel services. Similarly the problems which students face individually and at–large as a result of their inability to adjust to the curriculum, lead to the necessary consideration that possibly the curriculum itself and the all–school program have made operational conditions causing problems and frustrations which might best be eliminated through coordinated curriculum planning. Such an approach toward the development of the instructional program might build out rather than build in the problems with which counselors and school psychologists have frequently been saturated.

These are awarenesses which every curriculum supervisor should have in considering the broad ramifications of the instructional program and of his work with teachers. Curriculum supervisors must necessarily become involved with pupil personnel services in the areas of information in which they can contribute to the study of the actual effectiveness of the curriculum and the problems which the curriculum itself creates, or to which it contributes. When the curriculum supervisor to fail to realize the contributions which pupil personnel services make, particularly as manifested in the training and skills of the school psychologist and guidance counselor, he helps create a milieu of problems in the American public school of the kind which "THE COORDINATED APPROACH" attempts to remedy.

School psychology has become a field of considerable significance in recent years. School psychologists are being trained in ever increasing numbers to fill what appears to be a rapidly increasing demand for their services in the schools of this country. That school psychology has become so popular a field suggests that school psychologists have contributed something of value to education. However, this something of value leaves much room for improvement.

If the reader has had contact with a number of school psychologists, he will agree that each psychologist is likely to define his practicing role somewhat differently from his colleague. And it is well known that teachers and administrators perceive the functions of the school psychologist differently. But regarding one aspect there is agreement from all individuals. This concerns the fact that the school psychologist must be a positive force within the educational system, whether his contribution lies primarily in the area of individual testing, group testing, grade placement, therapy, research, teaching, program development or in-service. It should be clear, however, that if the psychologist functions as a school psychologist he must interpret his observations within the context of the school setting. Because of this, he is not simply a clinician although he must be clinically skilled.

Training in school psychology varies from setting to setting. Often the school psychologist is a person primarily clinically trained with "a few courses in education." Often his entry into school work indicates how naive he is with regard to what actually goes on in the classroom and in the cafeteria. Many of the criticisms directed at teachers regarding their difficulty in correlating what they know about human development with what they teach applies equally to psychologists, only with psychologists the problem lies in correlating what is taught with why the child responds as he does. The assumption in the former case is that teachers understand human development and in the latter case it is that psychologists understand curriculum.

The authors contend that the training of school psychologists has not enough emphasized the development of curriculum. In the relative failure to consider the problems of curriculum the school psychologist functions in a kind of vacuum. An example which comes to mind follows. Cursive writing is taught in many schools at the 3rd grade level, often being introduced toward the end of the 2nd grade. The justification for the introduction of cursive writing for all children at these levels escapes the authors. The often heard argument favoring introduction at this level is that parents expect the child to stop printing at this time and to begin to learn to write as an adult. Such reasoning suggests that parents have not only a great deal to say about school budgets, but also, even though they are laymen in education, they are authorities regarding curriculum and child development as this development concerns education. It should be apparent that the kind of motor control necessary for smooth cursive writing is beyond the ability of a great many children. Thus, these children learn poor writing habits which unfortunately are difficult to eradicate.

Concern with such problems is consistent with the school–related functioning of the school psychologist. Here is an opportunity to clearly define what the school psychologist has to offer that is not offered by other kinds of psychologists and is unlikely to be offered outside the school setting.

This means, however, that the training of the school psychologist must help him to correlate what he learns about growth and development whether this be physical, social, or emotional development, with the process of curriculum development. Goals ascribed to particular courses of study must be appropriate for the age level of the youngster, considering his interests and abilities. Any good remedial reading person will indicate the futility of struggling with the words of the 2nd grade reader, within the context of the 2nd grade story, when instructing a ten year old! It behooves the psychologist to become very familiar with the curriculum of his school and to evaluate repeatedly the extent of the relationship between that curriculum and the child to whom it is directed.

Another obvious example of the kind of involvement necessary in the correlation of curriculum and child development lies in an understanding of "sex differences." Many parents will confirm the observation that "boys are more difficult than girls to raise, especially as youngsters." It is an often noted observation that indeed there is a marked difference in the interests and abilities of boys and girls and that this difference becomes very apparent in school as early as kindergarten.

There appears to be a difference in fine–hand coordination, in language skills and speech development, in length of attention span and in such social behavior as politeness, conformity, and boisterousness. Yet, boys and girls are both registered in kindergarten at the same chronological age and exposed to the same kinds of experiences in the same order and at the same time. Undoubtedly, it will take considerable creativity and initiative on the part of school boards and school administration to change this situation. However, the dropout problem is often seeded in the primary grades.

Unless the school psychologist has something very special to offer the school, his functions can be eliminated at considerable saving to school boards. With the increased flow of federal funds to local mental health services, much of what too many school psychologists now call their functions can be comfortably performed by psychometricians and other mental health workers. But these workers cannot reach into the heart of the school because they do not have a working knowledge of curriculum or of the difficulties inherent in classroom teaching.

Obviously the authors contend that the role of curriculum in the training of school psychologists must be emphasized. They should be able to define a program of study to include its goals and objectives and the instructional techniques that apply to the particular group involved. It is not suggested that they become teachers or that they become curriculum coordinators. It is suggested that they have a more than nodding relationship with the problems of curriculum, a relationship predicated on the assumption that with this knowledge they can truly make a unique contribution to the schools they serve.

A second implication for the training of school psychologists arises from the position the school psychologist holds in serving as a liaison person between the school and some outside helping agency. Obviously, when the ophthalmologist sends a note to the school nurse–teacher asking her to notify the child's teacher that the child cannot see the blackboard unless he is sitting within ten feet of the board, a simple seating change is made and a possible potential learning problem is avoided. When an audiometer test finds a hearing loss of some significance, the same school nurse–teacher makes a home contact and she even notifies the family physician or the local speech and hearing clinic that a referral is on its way. Follow up is one of her major functions. The nurse–teacher is not simply a first aid man. Neither, we hope, is the school psychologist simply an I.Q. tester who fills the files with reports which mean little to teachers and often, not much more to other psychologists. As an effective and contributing school psychologist one of his functions is to educate outside school agencies to the contributions they can make to help the child within the school setting.

Psychiatric clinics often exist in isolation from the school in that they are not aware of the perhaps destructive quality of a child's behavior when this occurs within the classroom. For behavior to be destructive to the classroom, the only requirement is that it repeatedly draw the attention of the teacher and the pupils away from the focus of the class. This intrudes upon continuity and may inhibit communication of meaning.

There are times when school personnel and clinic personnel do not agree about the behavior or motivation or responsibility of the child common to both of them. What may be seen as a hopeful sign of emotional growth from one point of view may be seen as a worsening of the classroom situation from another point of view. It would seem that the child stands to benefit if the school psychologist can help the teacher and the clinic to an understanding of the total situation and the school psychologist can do this if he serves in a liaison capacity, respecting both the agencies he serves. His is a job of translation and again a job of coordination and correlation. He must be supportive of the needs of the teacher and of the aims of the clinic. If he cannot be, then it behooves him to call for a meeting of the involved persons.

If, within the training of the school psychologist, he can have the experience of playing this liaison role, of communicating with the child's physician, or with a clinic of one or another kind, he is in a position to educate people in roles significant yet tangential to that of the school, to what the school must ask of them for the ultimate benefit of the child. How often does a family physician or pediatrician write out a gym excuse when there is no valid reason, but simply a request from a protective parent. How often does this same physician, in a sincere effort to comfort the child's parents, comment about a school situation without knowledge of the circumstances. Since the mountain cannot (or will not?) come to Mohammed, Mohammed must make the move!

"THE COORDINATED APPROACH" has stressed coordination at all school levels for the development of a coordinated effort of education. Obviously, in the lesson learned through in-school coordination, there is a lesson to be learned outside the school. The school psychologist deals with a child who exists profitably, comfortably, or miserably both in the school and out of it. No matter how his behavior may differ in the school as contrasted with his behavior out of the school he is still the same child. That his behavior differs is undoubtedly meaningful, but a full understanding of what is going on, an understanding that will ultimately lead to a more comfortable and more successful school performance and adjustment, cannot be had without reaching outside of the school to at least some of those people who are significant to the child. This means that the school psychologist must reach out in many directions, from parents to clinics to physicians to tutors. He may see, he **will** see far fewer children over the school year, but he should be much more helpful to those he sees and in his contacts as liaison person with outside school agencies, he should be serving to educate over a broader spectrum. There are far too many people critical of schools, advising regarding school problems, who know little or nothing about school situations.

A third implication of "THE COORDINATED APPROACH" for the training of school psychologists lies in the necessity of helping prospective school psychologists to develop an empathic understanding of the teaching situation. Although there undoubtedly is much validity to the criticisms directed at many teachers, a teacher's job is by no means one to be taken lightly or to be considered an easy job. The teacher's responsibilities are many and it is often an exceedingly difficult task to understand thirty children well enough to motivate all of them even half of the time. Influences on children come from many directions and not all of these influences are catalytic to teaching or learning. Each day new materials pour in to be used, new knowledge is to be learned and assimilated, new problems develop to be faced. Since each class is quite different the teacher must make constant adjustment not only in the way he interacts with the class, but in the way he teaches. At the day's end, the teacher who has given considerably of himself is realistically exhausted. To be told by a school psychologist that he must do even more, that he must praise somehow and love somehow and understand—always understand, often leaves him with the feeling that it is not he who must do the understanding!

The authors do not feel that the school psychologist must be a trained teacher, but they do feel that a few weeks residence in a classroom as a student teacher would be of tremendous help to the school psychologist. Seeing first hand how difficult it is to meet everybody's needs, observing individual differences in action, seeing directly how children interact with each other and adult authorities, would contribute considerably to a broadening of the school psychologist's view of the role of the teacher. In addition, this short period within the classroom contributes also to a greater appreciation of the role of the principal and gives the school psychologist some insight into the way dicta filter down to the teacher.

Within the framework of "THE COORDINATED APPROACH" set forth here, the teacher is seen from a number of different views, as are other members of the school. It may be easier to stand somewhat removed from the teacher while dispensing with suggestions for improving the classroom climate, but it is suggested here that distance makes it also easier to breed misunderstanding and perhaps, resentment. Empathic relationship need not blind the school psychologist to the realities of poor teaching, but it should make it easier to communicate since communication can then take place within an understaning of the total situation.

A final implication of the approach presented in this text lies in an evaluation of the notion of "voluntary commitment." It was earlier suggested that the authors believed in-service to be more successful when attendance was voluntary. The reasons for this feeling need not be repeated here. Clinical psychologists and other mental health workers have indicated throughout the literature that the patient who voluntarily seeks help in solving his problems is far more likely to be better motivated toward therapy than the patient court-ordered or in some other way, pushed by someone outside himself, into a therapeutic intervention.

The child who is referred to the school psychologist generally has little or no choice about his referral. He enters into a relationship with the school psychologist because he has been directed to do so. Fortunately, his relationship with the school psychologist is generally pleasant, even though he may be facing for the first time the meaning of his behavior, or seeing that someone else knows what his behavior indicates about him. While he did not voluntarily come to the psychologist for help, the child has had considerable experience with authority within the school setting and more often than not, he bows to the authority as a matter of habit. His defiance is not likely to be overt in the great majority of cases.

With the child's parents the reaction may not be quite so docile. Many a school psychologist has experienced the hostility of parents "ordered" to see him because of a child's problems. Whatever the hostility may represent, whether it is parental self–protection, genuine concern on a realistic basis over an invasion of privacy, or simple misconception about the meaning of the referral, the parent called in to see the school psychologist did not make the first move himself. His appointment was not made because **he** sought help, but rather because a school official told him he had a problem which needed help.

The clinical training, then, of the school psychologist needs to take into consideration this very marked difference in the kind of first interview between the psychologist and the parent in the typical psychiatric or guidance clinic and the typical school setting. In the former situation the parent has made some kind of voluntary commitment to the recognition of a problem and he is now taking the second step since he is seeking help. In the latter situation the parent is being faced with his child's problems perhaps for the first time. There is much to be realized between the first notice of a problem that needs help and the actual move towards obtaining that help. And there is considerable difference in the kind of relationship existing between the parent who comes to the psychologist of his own volition and asks for help and the parent who is told he is to come to the psychologist and take help, regardless of the need existing for him.

There is a parallel to be drawn here. We all know people who are blind to their own weaknesses, to their needs for status, to their moral responsibilities, etc. But we cannot expect them to accept our help or our pearls of wisdom until they first develop an awareness of their need for this help. A resisting teacher forced to participate in a workshop or course of study he resents taking is not likely to profit markedly from his participation and there is the distinct possibility that his resentment will be communicable as if it were some kind of disease. He needs to be led to the first stage of awareness—that his need does in fact exist. So it is with the parent.

It cannot be forgotten in the training of the school psychologist that he must first help those sitting on the other side of his desk to an awareness that a problem needing help exists. This is often a most frustrating experience, not unlike the situation faced repeatedly by the teacher as he tries to teach a child unwilling to learn. It is a frustration every trainee should know well.

D. Implications of "THE COORDINATED APPROACH" for the United States Federal Government Public Education Programs for Rural and Urban Depressed Areas

Since 1965, the United States Federal Government has assumed an increasing responsibility and commitment toward American social progress which has strong ramifications for public education. Specifically, these ramifications have focused upon developing more effective public school programs in rural poverty areas and in the depressed, inner-city areas of large cities. The planning of programs and approaches to these problems has been based upon the recognition that the lower-lower class socio-economic orientation of populations in these areas is sufficiently deprived that the middle class value bases of public school programs in such settings is meaningless in terms of the experimental backgrounds of students.

Approaches being organized to develop public education programs designed to reach such students and their environment should seek to communicate in terms of values which the learners can understand and accept as applicable to them. Such programs must provide experiences for students which will allow them to meaningfully understand society at-large. With such an orientation, students will have an honest opportunity to gain skills, information and effective preparation from public school educative experience to compete in society at-large and raise their level of living and achievement. First among such approaches to be actualized is the Head Start pre-school program, designed to broaden the experiential knowledge of depressed area children so that formal school programs will be able to build from a defined social experience shared by these children.

Although this perception is long overdue, the authors concur that this recognition of need is a perception which may have dramatic effect if programs are realistically and carefully planned and instituted. The approaches to planning such experiences in actual school curriculum and the preparation of teachers through pre-and in-service education must be radically different from attempts of the past. If such differences are not provided, the ultimate results in terms of learning experiences of students will be as colossal a failure as school programs prior to 1965 have been, only much more expensive!

The authors submit that the basic philosophy and much of the program of "THE COORDINATED APPROACH" have critical implication for the development of educational programs designed to meet the admirable objectives of these federal government commitments. The planning of over-all objectives, local objectives, school and subject matter objectives must be cooperatively undertaken in a setting which realizes the actualities of the environmental need and experience of the students. This will require coordination of expertise from rural and urban sociology, ethnology, teacher education, and public school personnel. In local settings the involvement of the curriculum supervisor and school psychologists will be of crucial importance as they bring to their own school systems the general pattern planned for regional development.

While some regional in-service orientation and training of teachers and school personnel from schools may be developed, the job of working with teachers to develop the actual program for the local school will be a task which must be undertaken in a setting of close coordination of all of the services of that school. This in essence is a central objective of "THE COORDINATED APPROACH."

In the typical school setting, both the curriculum supervisor and psychologist will have heavy responsibility in working with teachers and students as new government sponsored programs are implemented in local and urban depressed area schools. "THE COORDINATED APPROACH", then, becomes as critical a factor in schools which will be involved in this program as the authors contend it can be in other school situations. The cooperative working together of the curriculum supervisor and school psychologist will offer the federal government programs in these school settings the advantage of coordinating all of the school's services in a preventive approach. It seems centrally important that the ultimate success of these government sponsored programs will be dependent upon identifying as early as possible, where re-working of ideas and programs must begin in terms of how students and teachers react to the new curricular experiences.

To assume that such programs will not need continuous analysis and evaluation for adjustment and refinement will be tragically shortsighted. We suggest that "THE COORDINATED APPROACH" offers a realistic and effective means to achieve this and at the same time orient the new programs to a preventive approach. Similarly, the authors contend that the basic ideas of coordination and articulation of the all-school program suggested in "THE COORDINATED APPROACH" have direct implications for the succinct and cooperative definition of objectives for such programs, their planning of in-service programs for school personnel and the development of basic curricular experiences for the programs by representatives from the areas of expertise mentioned earlier in this section.

The recognition of these problems by the federal government and its commitment to develop educational programs to ameliorate the problems, although overdue, is admirable. To approach the definition of these programs and to implement them in the same manner as existing inadequate school programs for the imporverished would be foolhardy. The federal government has taken the position that we can no longer afford the "luxury" of such dismal educational failures for people in these settings. Unless an effective process for planning and developing programs to break through the vacuum of non-communication in present programs is organized, the results will be the same!

Coordinating the efforts of federal funds with "know-how" to develop locally effective programs for impoverished areas must replace the "no-how" ineffectiveness of present programs. People are far more sophisticated than they ever have been and will be far more critical of educational waste than in the past. The expenditure of federal funds to develop educational programs for the impoverished which will only duplicate the failures of past programs would be a tragic waste not only of monies and human energy but of the precious time schools have to work with these children. The lack of meaning in the program of experiences offered by the school in poverty settings is obvious. Specifically, this lack of meaning has grown from the attempts of public school programs to impose middle class values upon students from a lower socio-economic class orientatation. This is, in a large sense, similar to the concern of "THE COORDINATED APPROACH" with the problems of lack of meaning in school programs in middle-class, non-impoverished areas. In this setting, typical school programs for low-average students have failed because they are essentially diluted average and college-type programs having no validity for them.

Regardless of the social class orientation of students, unless the program of the school develops something more meaningful and motivating than the imposition of values and experiences above and apart from the experiental background of the learner, the results will invariably be the same, leading to non-communication, boredom and failure!

If the federal government is to succèed in developing effective educational programs for the impoverished, the curricular experiences which will be organized and offered must seek to communicate that which they have to offer through the common denominator of the shared experience of the learners. This means that we cannot impose our values and experiences as before, changing them ever so slightly or, as in the non-regents program, "watering down" the curriculum and school program. School programs, concrete and meaningful in terms of the environment of the student, must be defined and organized.

The end goals of educational programs for the impoverished will be much the same as programs in middle class environments. However, the jump from beginning to end in the environment of poverty is far too broad for the majority of learners to comprehend and accept. The end objectives are so far removed from the learner's experience and so abstract from his own environment that he rejects them because of their remoteness and because he cannot see how he can ever achieve them. To counteract this, new sets of **vital** and **immediate** objectives, objectives which are so concrete that you "can taste them," must be developed to provide a continuum for the learner to reach toward the end objectives of a better life for himself.

Educational programs for the impoverished, like all optimally successful educational experiences, **must** help the learner establish a personal objective in his learning toward which he will work and which he can achieve in the immediate setting. The planning of curriculum in these settings should provide not only for the personal achievement of the learner in his accomplishment, but a socially desirable achievement as well. Curricula in such programs should seek to identify Major Social Functions[1] and Persistent Life Situations[2] for the learners in their own environment. If the excitement of meaning for students has been built into the general education learnings of the primary grades, the programs in intermediate and early secondary school years may be able to transcend such interests into the larger world of society at-large. Before these later experiences can be approached with meaning, however, we must help students define and achieve their immediate personal objectives in school programs. This achievement must provide sufficient success and reward that the next objective will be defined and pursued.

Each of these steps of objective definition and achievement should be little anticipatory responses leading to and anticipating the larger and final objectives of the educational sequence. While all of these are small they are directed toward the student's individual and social development consistent with the larger objective of realistic and creative contribution to the broad society. It has been the lack of such channels for progress and self-realization in a context of student's environment and experience which has characterized the past failure of educational programs in impoverished

[1]Hollis L. Caswell and Doak S. Campbell, **Curriculum Development,** New York, The American Book Company, 1935, pp. 173–186.

[2]Florence B. Stratemeyer, Hamdem Forkner, Margaret McKim, and Harry Passow, **Developing A Curriculum For Modern Living,** second edition, revised, New York Bureau of Publications, Teachers College, Columbia University, 1957, pp. 155–182.

areas. The achievement of each step should bring students' perceptions closer toward identifying personal and societal meaning within the context of his own life plans. The collective total organization of these steps should be the curriculum of the school program for the impoverished. As examples of the context of experiences and environment of students in impoverished areas we would cite the following. The study of a health curriculum which encourages the juice, cereal, bacon and eggs, toast and milk breakfast for children who consider themselves lucky to find a piece of dried bread to nibble in the morning has little validity or meaning. While the learner may pass the test in the unit by putting down such a desired response for the question, his breakfast habits are not liable to change from the dried bread unless as an adult he has gained the earning power and the social values which make this possible and desirable. The latter two achievements are, hopefully, what his education may help him gain. In the meantime, the teacher's criticism of eating the dried slice of bread because it isn't nutritional does little to satiate the hunger that drives the student to eat it. Such "learning activities" are meaningless academic questions and only teach the student who lives with this hunger that his teacher has not yet learned "a bird in the hand is worth two in the bush!" The juice, cereal, bacon and eggs, toast and milk breakfast is a far more unrealistic and unattainable objective for most impoverished children than the blythe teacher with his naive health program will ever realize!

The poverty stricken child needs to learn to read but not initially to read about a middle class world in which he cannot even fantasy himself. His own environmental needs to read are critically important to the point of life and death but are typically not noticed by the school. This child needs to learn to read and understand the meaning of "danger" and "poison" on cans of rat poison, "pure" and "safe" on other containers. Other things to be read and understood include signs on condemned buildings with words and expressions like "condemned," "under razing," "structure not safe," "symptoms of rabies are:," but the reading materials used in class talk about a boy, a girl and their dog and **their** environment in all-caucasian suburbia. The poverty stricken child needs to learn how to write but not how to write a business letter or invitations to a party. Pen pals in foreign lands similarly offer little incentive to learn writing but a shopping list or a fan letter to a popular music or sports idol may tap a need or interest.

Such suggestions may be taken by some as setting objectives and activities far too low. If this would prove true, the experiences gained in planning programs and activities at such a low level would allow the educational personnel to raise this level gradually higher until the response of students indicated that interests and environments were being reached. Such success has not been achieved by moving typical programs downward and the watering down of programs which never could communicate to non–middle class students has diluted them into form without any substance at all!

Educational programs for impoverished areas in the past have given nothing but lip service to the maxim that "you take the child where he is" and begin his education there if you wish to be effective. The proposed federal programs will achieve this effectiveness, only if they are willing and able to recognize and accept impoverished children for what they are and define and organize programs of education which will begin where they can comprehend them. Physically and societally, they are barely clothed, poorly nurtured, not sweet–smelling and not too motivated to learn our ways. If we take these children where they are, we must start with an awareness and acceptance of their needs and set our objectives initially at the bottom rung of **their** ladder. In teaching them to climb the first step we must make the steps small, allow them to define their goals and climb the first step, enjoy and realize their achievement and help them to want to try another step. Hopefully, such an approach will cause them to climb up the ladder and out of the cistern of poverty, the only environment they have known. Once out of the cistern, society at–large can be meaningfully considered, its scope understood, and plans made to effectively enter into it. Rewards for such learners must be tangible. Objectives such as food, warmer clothes, a bed, a room, and "no cough" must be defined and steps to achieve them planned which will be rewarding for them individually and for society at–large. Education must provide something for the impoverished that they want to achieve and which will be a learning experience for them.

To be effective, educational programs for the impoverished must begin considering the cause rather than the symptom. This failure to attack the cause in educating such people has been a contributor to the following situations, both of which have sought to be socially remedial without giving consideration to societal development and readiness.

Urban renewal projects in city settings today have sought to revitalize obsolete and depressed, inner–city areas. In many instances, the housing in the blight areas was dangerous and unhealthy. The new structures in many of these "renewed areas," however, have been beyond the financial reach of former blight area occupants. Other impoverished residents of the former blight area are fearful of going into the new and threatening middle–class environment. Both causes have often resulted in these impoverished people moving into areas adjacent to the renewed district which are becoming blight areas themselves. The people who have eventually reinhabited the renewed area are people who can afford or choose to move there but who were not the impoverished people it was hoped the urban renewal project would help. Their plight, in such instances, has not been ameliorated. They have only moved to another area which is in a process of increasing decline either because it is all they can afford or because, although unpleasant and uncomfortable, it is familiar to them and not something unknown and, threatening.

Other unfortunate situations have arisen where federally supported apartment complexes have been developed for impoverished people. Numerous instances of ignorance and mishandling of the facilities of such units by impoverished people, as new tenants, have been recorded. Throwing sewage out of windows into the apartment courts instead of using lavatory facilities and piling garbage in the apartment hallways instead of using the kitchen sink garbage disposals were widespread occurances because the tenants had not previously had such facilities. With instruction and orientation such practices have decreased and the facilities have been increasingly used as intended.

The mere provision of facilities is no guarantee that they will be utilized wisely or that they will really be any improvement in people's way of life. Of course, the implications for adult education here are tremendous, but the point at hand is how federal government commitment to developing effective public school programs for the impoverished can be facilitated. Good intentions must be bourne out by effective, meaningful planning as to how these objectives can be actualized and achieved. The advantages and economy of frozen foods, although numerous, are of no value to a person who is unaware of, uninterested in or unable to afford a food freezer or rent freezer locker space. Similarly the objective of giving people grain to plant so they can raise a crop to provide for future grain needs is lost if the people are so hungry that they have to eat the seed sent for planting because they are starving.

Likewise, the impoverished child must be given an educational program which will teach him to read first for **life,** then for luxury. Teach him money concepts and **then** number concepts. To be successful, such programs will require succinct definition of objectives, curricular sequences built upon life experiences of the children and their families in their experiential environment and preparation of teachers in pre and in-service settings in the field, not solely in classrooms. "THE COORDINATED APPROACH" in essence advocates knowing students in terms of motivation, interests, culture and intelligence and the building of educational programs upon these characteristics of the students as opposed to directing students in terms of a value system foreign to them and built upon pre-conceived, structured subject matter.

◆◆◆◆

IN RETROSPECT

"THE COORDINATED APPROACH" has sought to develop a continuous operational philosophy of cooperation among the general and special services existing in the American public school today. Its primary objective is to develop an awareness which will lead to a more realistic and more comprehensive approach to meaningful curriculum planning with an emphasis upon organizing all-school programs which will be preventive in their orientation. At the same time, "THE COORDINATED APPROACH" seeks to build out problems for students and teachers which presently are treated by tardy diagnosis and therapeutics. The facilities, resources, and services necessary to implement this philosophy presently exist in a majority of American school systems. All that is necessary to effect it is a sincere desire to do so.

BIBLIOGRAPHY

Caswell, Hollis L., and Campbell, Doak S., **Curriculum Development,** New York, The American Book Company, 1935.

Focusing Teacher Preparation in Teaching Center Schools, Inter-University Project One Sponsored by the Ford Foundation, State University of New York at Buffalo, Buffalo, New York, 1965.

Krug, Edward A., **Curriculum Planning,** Revised Edition, New York, Harper and Brother, 1957.

Stratemeyer, Florence B., Forkner, Hamden L., McKim, Margaret A., and Passow, A. Harry, **Developing a Curriculum for Modern Living,** Second Edition, Revised, New York, Bureau of Publications, Teachers College, Columbia University, 1957.

NOTES

NOTES

Photo Composition / Design – STUDIO 701, INC., 701 SENECA ST., BUFFALO, N.Y. 14210

NOTES

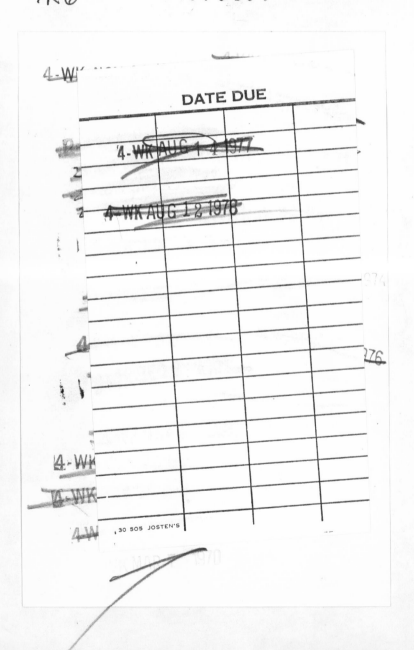